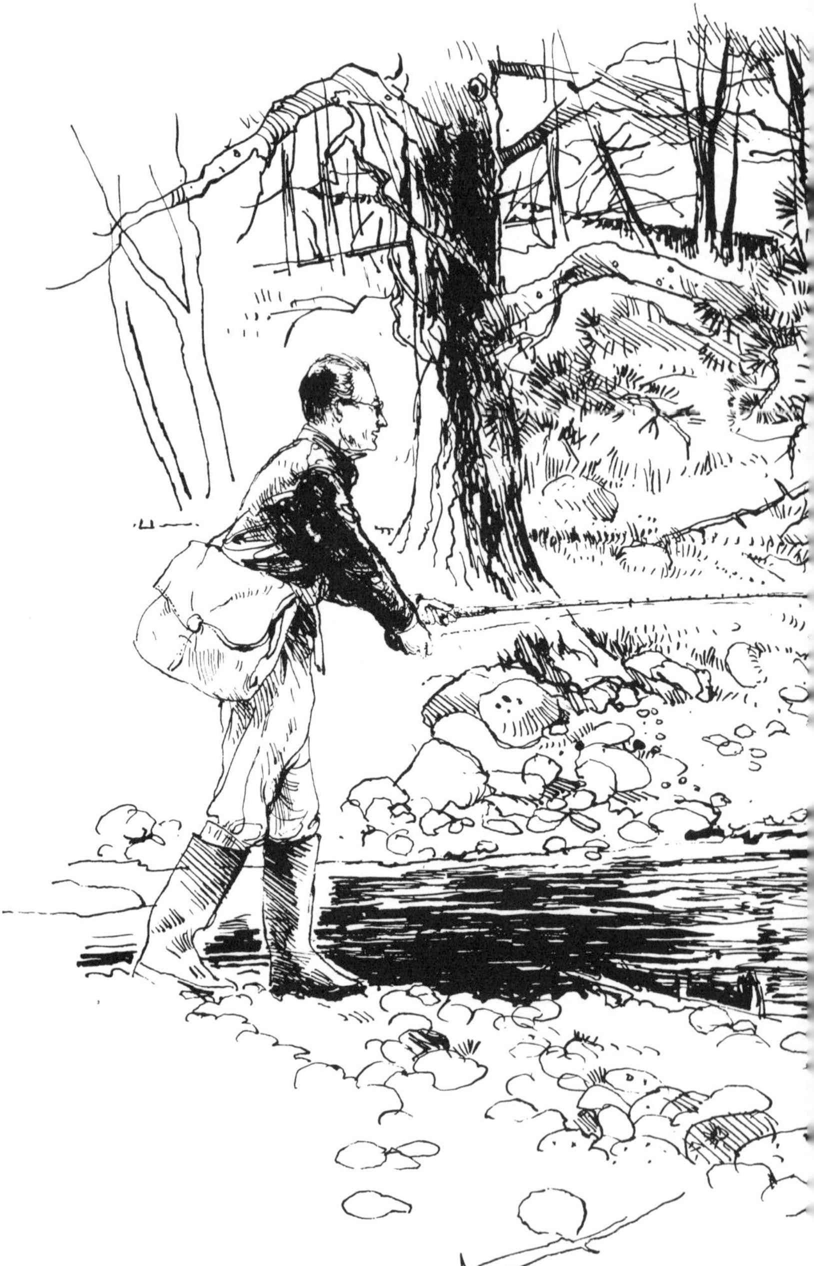

JOHN INGLIS HALL

FISHING
A
HIGHLAND STREAM

A LOVE AFFAIR WITH A RIVER

VIKING

VIKING

Published by the Penguin Group
27 Wrights Lane, London w8 5TZ, England
Viking Penguin Inc., 40 West 23rd Street, New York, New York 10010, USA
Penguin Books Australia Ltd, Ringwood, Victoria, Australia
Penguin Books Canada Ltd, 2801 John Street, Markham, Ontario, Canada L3R 1B4
Penguin Books (NZ) Ltd, 182–190 Wairau Road, Auckland 10, New Zealand

Penguin Books Ltd, Registered Offices: Harmondsworth, Middlesex, England

First published by Putnam & Co. Ltd 1960
Published by Viking 1987
Reprinted 1987, 1988

Copyright © John Inglis Hall, 1960
Foreword copyright © Geoffrey Cox, 1987
Illustrations copyright © Gavin Rowe, 1987

All rights reserved. Without limiting the rights under copyright reserved
above, no part of this publication may be reproduced, stored
in or introduced into a retrieval system, or transmitted, in any form
or by any means (electronic, mechanical, photocopying,
recording or otherwise), without the prior written permission of both
the copyright owner and the above publisher of this book

Photoset in 10/12 Linotron Aldus by
Rowland Phototypesetting Ltd
Bury St Edmunds, Suffolk
Printed in Great Britain by
William Clowes Ltd
Beccles and London

British Library Cataloguing in Publication Data
Hall, John Inglis
How to fish a highland stream: a love letter to a river.
—(Viking sports and pastimes)
1. Trout fishing—Scotland 2. Fly fishing—Scotland
I. Title
799.1'755   SH688.G7
ISBN 0-670-81473-3

Library of Congress Catalog Card No.: 87-50538

CONTENTS

Foreword by Sir Geoffrey Cox 7
1. THE CHOICE 11
2. A WOMAN BUT NOT A LADY 17
3. HOW THE LAND LIES 21
4. INDUCTION 26
5. A DISTRACTING BAY 31
6. FIRST TRUE DAY 36
7. THE APPROACH 43
8. THE FINE-SPUN PORTRAIT I 52
9. THE FINE-SPUN PORTRAIT II 65
10. ERICHT DIVERSION 86
11. THE FINE-SPUN PORTRAIT III 95
12. HOT DAY AT CUAICH 112
13. THE FINE-SPUN PORTRAIT IV 117
14. THE LAST POOL 124

FOREWORD

There are places which it is possible to love as deeply as if they were people. *Fishing a Highland Stream* by John Inglis Hall is an account of one man's love for a small river, the Truim, in the Central Scottish Highlands, its countryside and inhabitants. Feeling and sincerity make it a minor classic, not only about trout fishing but about nature, portraying both the lure and the art of fly fishing, and the fascination of the ancient, ice-eroded mountains of the Cairngorms.

I came upon the book by chance, some time after I had fallen in love with the Truim myself and experienced the lonely magic of its route, in those days in a glen where only the grazing roe deer and the shrill oyster-catchers watched your passing. Before long, I began to take it with me in my fishing bag, wrapped in a plastic cover, partly to gather points and perceptions from the author's methods, but also to see the river with his eyes as well as my own. With him, I came to look for 'the identical, unchanging, permanent duty owl on guard at the mouth of the Truim', the stretch above the Laggan Bridge where the water 'glitters and is shade-dappled', and the bend near the electricity pylons, which is 'fished to the sound of music' as the wind plays upon 'this great harp we have stretched across the moors'.

It remains a place of remembered hidden corners to which my wife and I try to make an annual pilgrimage on our way to rivers farther North. Once a year, too, I re-read the book, not only for the Truim itself, and the Dalwhinnie country, but for John Inglis Hall's feeling and superbly expressed regard for it. It is good to think that this new edition will bring pleasure like my own to many other people, not only fishers, but to all those who love the life and landscape of places set apart.

Sir Geoffrey Cox
1987

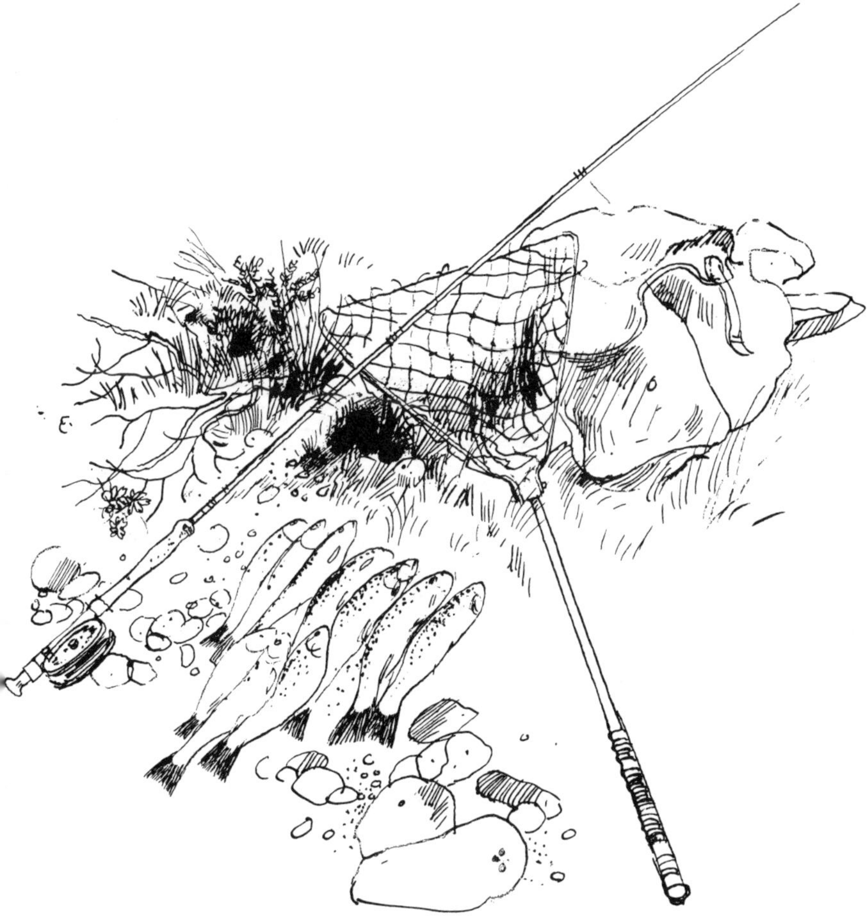

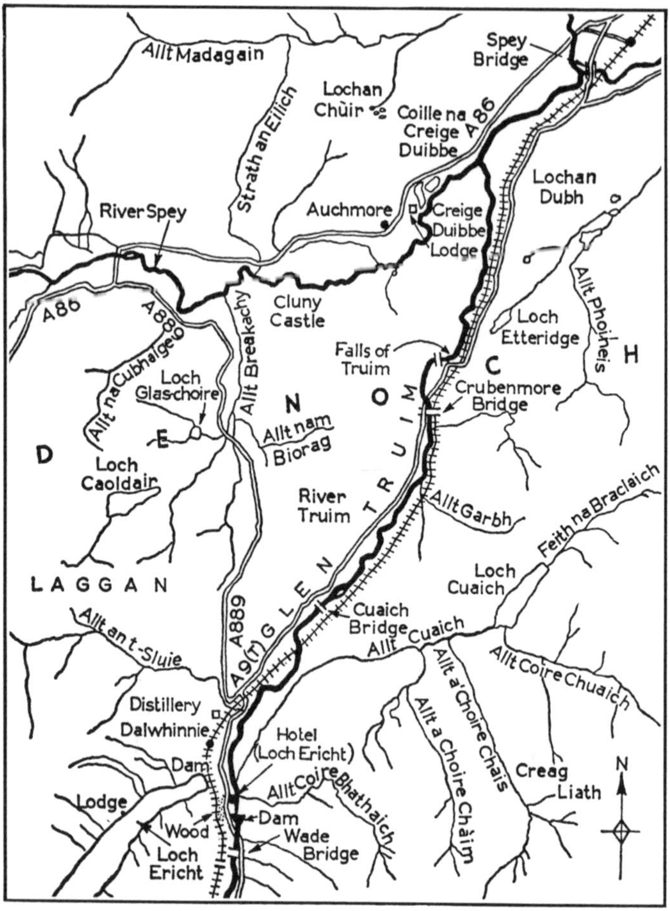

Allt Madagain
Strath an Eilich
Lochan Chùir
Coille na Creige Duibbe
A86
Spey Bridge
Lochan Dubh
River Spey
Auchmore
Creige Duibbe Lodge
Cluny Castle
A86
A889
Allt na Cubhaige
Allt Breakachy
Loch Etteridge
Allt Phoineis
Falls of Truim
Crubenmore Bridge
Loch Glas-choire
Allt nam Biorag
D E N O C H
Loch Caoldair
River Truim
Allt Garbh
Feith na Braclaich
GLEN TRUIM
LAGGAN
Loch Cuaich
Cuaich Bridge
Allt Cuaich
A889
A9(T)
Allt an t-Sluie
Allt a' Choire Chais
Allt Coire Chuaich
Allt a Choire Chàim
Distillery
Dalwhinnie
Hotel (Loch Ericht)
Dam
Allt Coire Bhathaich
Creag Liath
N
Lodge
Wood
Dam
Wade Bridge
Loch Ericht

1

THE CHOICE

As in marriage, so in fishing; one's choice is made by accident. One opens the door of a room; and there, for better or for worse, the lady sits. One sees a river from a train, a car, one halts to stretch one's legs and is lost.

My long affair with the Truim – we are not married, in spite of temperamental differences which make us ideally suited – has been a delight to me. But the role of mistress is also an honourable one; and anyway, wife-river or mistress-river, we met by accident.

It happened like this. About ten years ago I was ill in the summer and had to be three weeks away in the autumn to refresh myself before returning to work. I had not fished trout in Scotland save for a short time while commando-training in the Western Highlands during the war, and decided to go back to the Highlands for those three weeks. Instead of following my own good nose to the lochs and burns in the forest and moorland country round Loch Morar, Mallaig and Arisaig that I had fished as I steered my erratic apprentice compass courses under the cold spring rain of 1944, I asked a too-wise Scottish friend where I should fish, where the best Highland trout fishing was to be found. With him began the series of mistakes which finally landed me late one stormy September evening at Dalwhinnie on the Truim.

My friend was infinitely knowledgeable. He weighed up place after place, most learnedly, and finally sent me to an hotel and a river, the names of which for Shylock's wilderness of monkeys I would not reveal, which for me was absolutely, but as it turned out not irretrievably, wrong. It was a fine hotel that had once been a Laird's house; the river was a beauty to look at from the hill on which the hotel stood, but when you went down to it at almost every pool there was at least one person worming for extremely wary and rather tired red salmon. The hotel, too, at that season, was full of shooting people; nobody was interested in fishing or fishermen; dinners in the evening were long and formal. Furthermore, my fishing costume and equipment tend to resemble the campaigning rig of the White Knight in *Through the Looking-Glass*, and I felt at once that the shooters were a little out of place with their serious moorland chic and the elegant country dress which seemed for them mandatory. I worried lest they should feel diminished socially by a man who dined in waders, and on my second evening found myself considering over my cheese soufflé how I might get away. In the meantime I had caught two, I thought, slightly disillusioned seatrout and one small brown trout. The salmon would not as much as glance at my fly; the moment they saw it was neither a worm nor a triangle they were apparently satisfied that I was a visitor and therefore perfectly harmless, and I could splash about as much as I liked. But move they would not.

So after dinner I telephoned to my wife and asked her to send me a wire saying that my grandmother was ill and would I come home at once. The next day I left in an aura of sympathy and regret which made me feel deceitful, though I paid cheerfully the forfeit for my booked room. The fact was that I had seen a place from the train on the way up, a nice desolate place of bare hills; bald, heather-tinted and treeless, with a blue stormy loch beating against a long white concrete dam by the railway line, a grey slate-roofed hotel half hidden behind a conifer spinney, a river only broad as a trickling burn, and a bleak, trim railway station, the two lines spanned by an old iron footbridge, with the name

Dalwhinnie, square and uncompromising, done in white, on a grey signboard. We had spun through it at around six-thirty in the morning after the cheerful run downhill from the Pass of Drumochtar. It was a fine morning, the only one I saw there that year, and for me at once there had been something magical about the place. The air had a bite to it, but not a chill. It was exquisitely clear, so that the whole landscape had the appearance of being washed utterly clean and free from taint of sin. The wet webs of spiders glittered among the heather in the slant of the early sun.

But at that time I was going somewhere else and, as every true fisherman must tell himself when he has to pass by a fancied place, somewhere better. I saw the loch – I found it was called Loch Ericht on my map – disappear and watched from the train the meagre river since, for a time, the railway line runs alongside it, then went down to the dining car to my porridge and bacon and egg, and thought no more about it though the name Dalwhinnie, unknown to me, had slipped quietly into my subconscious; registered as a conifer copse and a grey hotel, hills and a great blue loch, wind-ruffled in the clear of the morning, seen from the train. So after failure in the first grand place, inevitably, that was where I decided to go; and I went.

The train stopped at around eight in the evening; a long heavy sleeper train, London bound, with two stertorous engines, in tandem, to pull it up the gradient to Drumochtar. It was towards dusk and this evening there was no shine and glitter in the air, only greyness and an icy wind, gusting and dragging at all things movable. The rain was lashing down from low clouds moving fast as blown smoke. They covered the tops of the hills. I splashed through the shallow standing pools on the platform to the swinging station gate, showed my ticket and asked the stationmaster the name of the hotel by the conifer spinney, was given it and shouldered my bag and rods to walk the quarter-mile to it. On the way, despite the rain, the cold air drew pleasantly into the lungs. It tasted good and I liked it. I remembered that the map showed Dalwhinnie as lying at 1,100 feet; there was the explanation.

It was called the Loch Ericht Hotel. Over the light-brown door were the words in small black print, 'proprietor D. C. Matheson'. I pushed my bags and rods into the porch, shut out the rattling wind behind me, and went through the fire-warmed lounge, with its stuffed golden eagle and mounted specimen trout in glass cases, into the passageway on to which it gave, lugging my own things. A line of macintoshes, thick coats,

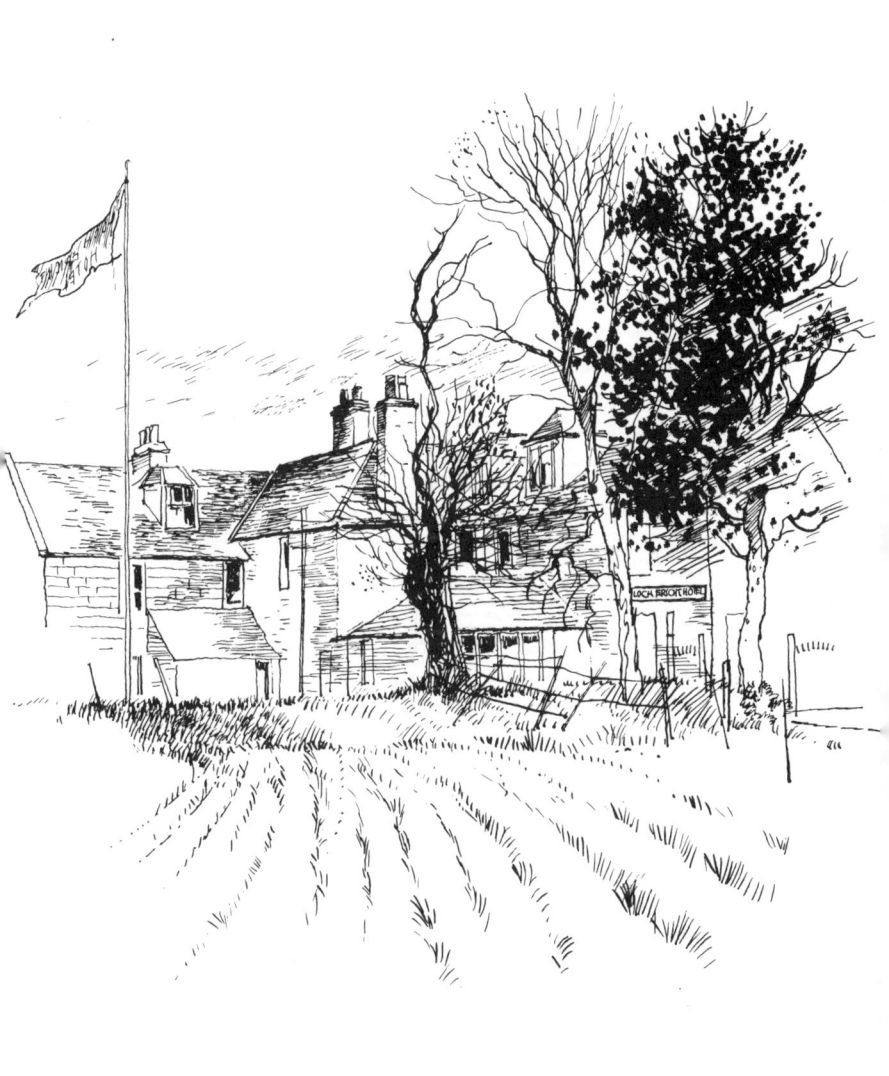

deer-stalker hats and crooked sticks hung on hooks on part of the wall to the right. Stairs to the left led to the upper floors.

'You want a room?'

A big man in brown tweeds, growing stout, quiet-spoken, reserved yet sure of himself, had come out of a sitting-room on the right marked 'private' and was greeting me.

I said I did, for a week, to fish.

'It's late in the season,' he said in true highland non-committal style, 'but you might try the loch. Yes, you might get something there, but I don't know.'

This was obviously the D. C. Matheson whose name was above the door. One of his sons carried my luggage and my rods upstairs, and I followed. I had a big room with two beds in it. I unpacked, then went down to tea. There seemed to be no other fishers in the hotel. This looked bad. Nobody in the house or on the staff said much to me; after all, I was seemingly a passer-by, a transient, and people who pass by generally don't mean very much. Very few stay and become part of a place. Besides, highlanders do not at once give themselves, and they may be right. It may be best to wait if there is to be friendship, for the two sides to reconnoitre, and prove themselves, the one to the other.

With Mr Matheson and his family it took perhaps two years until we were truly easy with one another, completely knit as friends; but there was a recognition of affinity very early, and the probationary two years were happy too.

My first night in the Matheson house was dreamlessly comfortable in a broad bed, just the right compromise between hard and soft, in which I found a hot stone bottle. I learned a few years afterwards that Queen Victoria and her Prince Consort Albert once stayed the night in that room; but their ghosts did not walk.

A WOMAN BUT NOT A LADY

I suppose I shall write about the Truim as though it were a story river instead of a real river of flesh and blood. In any event this can scarcely be avoided, for the eye of the beholder, which allocates beauty like an accolade, invents much about a river anyway, just as it invests with magic even an unworthy loved one. The fact is that anyone who reads about the Truim and sees it through my eyes must be very careful indeed not to be deceived.

It occurs to me that it might be fairer if I pointed out right away its defects, for these, with considered care, I invariably conceal from myself, but I have come to notice that they are serious enough entirely to defeat many people who have been lured by my jack o' lantern enthusiasm to give it a try. What follows then is a highly prejudiced man's attempt to be sensible, and not deceive to excess.

How to begin?

Perhaps by declaring first that the Truim is a damned contrary, difficult, cold, windswept little burn that habitually looks as though it would rise an inch if you spat in it. Secondly that much of it lies in a desolate broad valley, nearly treeless and more utterly exposed than any stream I know well. Thirdly that the wind blows harder gales and more bitterly, generally downstream, than the prevailing wind on any other river I fish. Fourthly that it rains habitually and torrentially a great deal of the time you are there; and if, as I do, you fish dry fly and wear glasses, the rain is lashed straight in your face by the wind.

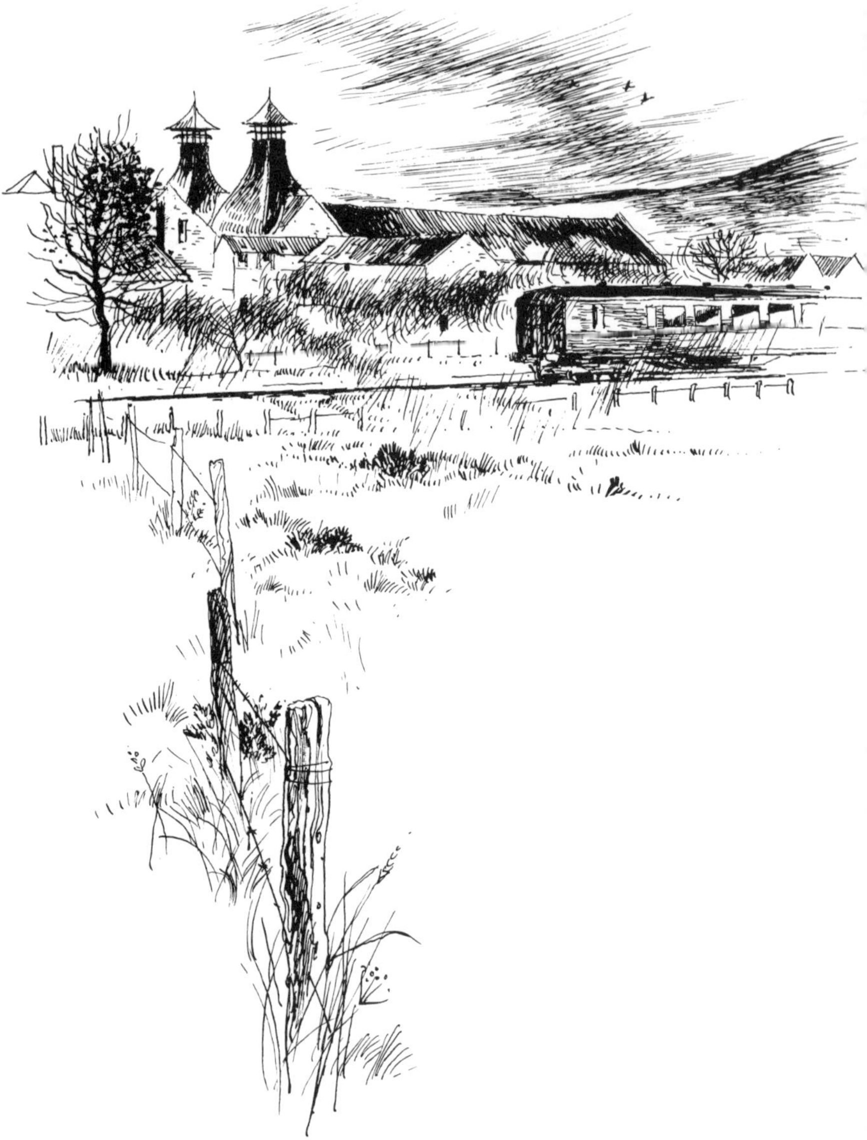

A WOMAN BUT NOT A LADY

Fifthly, it is perfectly capable of snowing in Dalwhinnie in May – or even June for that matter. So I invariably go prepared for Eskimo weather, with waterproof. The James Buchanan's Distillery in the village and good solid food in the hotel provide the other means of survival.

What else? Having declared broadly that the Truim is a woman but not a lady, 'uncertain, coy and hard to please', I must make it plain that it is not the river for anyone used to easy fishing or able to pay to fish the best aristocratic rivers. It is essentially a sample of that enormous, infinitely variable genus, the Scottish burn in hard country, as good or as bad as it is painted. Possibly the only point of this book may turn out to be as a guide to burn fishing and how to do it.

But this is presumption; everybody knows how to fish a burn. You fish downstream in water clear as a diamond, running your wet flies down the stickles and pools and dragging them towards you gently with small switching movements of the rod; you, the fisher, out of sight as far as possible, standing far back, if possible. Anyhow, the point is, I don't think, in fact I know, that this is not the best way to catch the trout there are in a burn at all.

Nobody can now say I have not warned them that the Truim is absolutely and by no means what an old Irish ghillie I knew called 'a gentleman's river'. In fact, let us be clear; it is in nine cases out of ten and for most of the year a difficult river in which to catch fish. It can be done, as my own record in the Loch Ericht Hotel fishing book shows, but only by being ready to fish ten hours a day without intermission, in any kind of weather but mostly bad. You also need to be a good fisherman. It is no place for beginners or those who are not really hard-bitten. I am.

HOW THE LAND LIES

The land makes the river; or rather the land makes the whole watershed. Part of the pleasure of fishing, for me, is to be aware remotely, with an atavistic feeling for events millennia before man, of how it was long, long ago; and to consider, with fascination, the thousands of later, changeless years, while my favoured river, still nameless, flowed, waiting for me as it now waits for others.

Round Dalwhinnie in the late Silurian and Devonian periods, roughly 275 to 330 million years ago, unspeakably huge volcanic upheavals raised in Scotland mountains as high as the Himalayas. This I always remember as I look at the bare, wild, low, smooth-rounded Cairngorms. The memory of the more magnificent peaks of which they are the worn stumps is as dear to me as anything connected with the countryside of today. I live, impossibly, in the uninhabited past as well as in the inhabited present when I fish Loch Ericht, or the Truim or the Spey, or any of the dozens of lochs and lochans hidden in the clefts and troughs in the surrounding hills and valleys. To do this is, I think, a part of complete enjoyment. Many others surely feel the same. It may be among the main, hidden reasons why the pleasure of mountain country is so great for those who love it.

Loch Ericht, which is a deep ditch in the hills, some sixteen miles long, lies almost due north-east. The railway line northwards to Inverness, sixty miles away, passes within 200 yards of its northernmost point. From there, you look straight down the loch to Benalder Bay, three miles away, backed by a dark green hump covered with conifers. The wind blows so hard between the loch's high, mountain banks that it is almost always ruffled. The high waves have a deep-troughed, vicious quality to them which has drowned many unwary, and even wary, men. The Truim itself flows down from above Drumochtar which is the next valley to the one that contains Ericht. It starts, a thin translucent trickle, and gathers force slowly; and even at its end where it flows into the Spey three-quarters of a mile below the Laggan Bridge on the road to Kingussie, it never amounts to very much. There are hundreds of burns like it all over Scotland.

The land through which it flows – I think, thousands of years ago, it contained a shallow or a deep lake in the part between Loch Ericht and the Bridge of Crubenmore – is also familiar. Stony, thankless, sheep country, heather-covered, with coarse grass on the thinnest of topsoils, the river bed is all smooth stones and rocks. For much of the year the water is a tenuous thread, and it runs very quickly away after a flood. In a dry season there will be very little fishing at all, because it runs down so fast that the trout mysteriously vanish among the boulders and pools and either are not seen, or if seen, are sluggish and inert, lying almost motionless, as though suspended, waiting for the freshening rain. Oxygen very easily fails them in so small and stony a stream.

The water when the river contains a good supply tastes delicious, certain though I am that it receives at various points untreated sewage and that animals die in it at will, or rather against their will. One does not drink near Truim's only city, Dalwhinnie, or near houses, nor perhaps should one drink Scottish river water to excess at any time, but drink one can when it is well oxygenated, and the Truim usually is. I have always done it and flourished. The delicate stomach may do what it will; I for one at least start level with the fish and my mouth, like theirs, appreciates the taste of their stream as well as its translucence and the disturbance of the wind on its ruffled surface.

The lower reach of the river, the reasoning fisher would expect, should be more protected from the wind. A mile below Crubenmore lie the Falls of Truim, where it narrows into a deep rocky cut, all dark swirling pools, white-edged with foam. Beyond it the river runs mostly through escarpments, sometimes as precipitously banked as railway cuttings, closely invested with dwarf oaks, birch, ash, fir, conifers, rowan and hazel sallies. The level of the river falls very quickly all the way. One would suppose that this hiding in a deep valley would signify a slight break in the cold after the five-mile moorland stretch upstream from Crubenmore to Dalwhinnie; that the wind would be less keen. This, however, is one of the things a man chilled to the bone on the upper reach tells himself for his comfort as he decides to move down to what he hopes may be more sheltered territory. The wind blows as keenly there, and can be almost more vicious. It seems to veer and blow dead into your face whichever way the river twists, as though the escarpments funnelled and channelled the wind, sucking it down from the upper air, always turning it, gusty and rain-laden, straight in your face. In this area, too, you are worse off than in the upper stretch in another way, for the river is in parts badly treed, and you need luck as well as skill to prevent yourself from being constantly hitched and hooked to the varied, attentive overhanging branches.

The real difference between the upper and lower reaches is not so much a difference between wind and wind; it is maddening on either. The difference is often, in spite of their nearness to one another, between weather and weather. Some days you find Dalwhinnie has had quite a different colour and quality of day to the deeper valley below Crubenmore: generally a little colder, a little wilder, a little harsher, but in any case the difference is never much – a degree or two in temperature, a few miles an hour in the speed of the wind, and for fishing, that is of no account.

There is another difference though: in late May and early June the primroses sometimes come out on the lower stretch so thickly that when you sit down on a rock to eat your lunch you paddle in primroses, your bags and tackle crush them, your eyes dazzle with the yellow. On the upper reach they lie less thickly.

4

INDUCTION

Nothing of what I have written in the previous chapter, however, was known to me when I woke up on my first morning in Dalwhinnie. In fact, truth to tell, I did not really take to the Truim until my third year visiting the place. I only awoke to the rain sweeping hard against my window, and a sense of well-being. To be warm in bed and listen to rain is a pleasure to be savoured, so I lay voluptuously and listened. When the gusts of wind dropped and the raindrop-patter grew for a moment less insistent, I could also hear the sound of the stream. It flows behind the hotel no more than twenty yards from the bedrooms, a continual reminder to fishermen to get fishing, to get up early and fish; or at night, before sleeping, that the river will be there in the morning.

When I went out after breakfast to try the loch, there was a curious deceptiveness about the weather in the yard in front of the hotel by the road. The breakfast-room wing with the porch alongside it is a buttress against the prevailing wind. Though it ruffles your hair, and across the road in the wood you can guess its strength by watching the sway of the trees, except on very cold days the air near the hotel seems to have a breath of mildness in it, as though the warmth of kitchen and clothes-drying room, bathroom tank and coal fire, act as a small stationary gulf stream warming a little the cold air and making a restricted temperate zone by the roadside. Leaving, one is of course full of food, which helps, but in the yard, out of the edge of the wind, the rain at first seems gentle and warm, as it was on my first day.

I put on my waders, gathered sandwiches from a plated tray in the hall, and put up my rod outside. Mr Matheson watched me go without much comment. It was evidently not very likely that I would do much good so late in the season. All he said, in a dubious voice, was:

'Well, I hope you do well.'

I pushed across the road and through the wood, sensing the rising wind. At the bridge under the railway line it was cold, but as I walked I sang a little. This is something I only allow myself in good open country where the sound is quickly absorbed; to listen to it is, I believe, an unusually awful musical experience, so I am, out of delicacy and consideration for others, no city singer. That morning the curlews came down to see what it was, then, aghast, took to the hills.

To the right under the bridge lies a small pool about fifty yards long by thirty wide which was a hole that the rain filled and refilled during the building of the Ericht Dam a few hundred yards away. It is named privately Loch Grant, for Donald Grant, a ghillie and a great countryman whom I have come to know well, who is dear to me and with whom I have passed many happy days. He introduced fingerling trout into Loch Grant, and so began the train of circumstances which led to its naming. Today, their descendants, mostly small because of the restricted space, take the fly greedily. It is the place where one catches most easily baits for trolling in Ericht for the great lake trout, the Ferox, but in it also there are several old cannibals who are well over the pound, and one, I think, over two.

Down on the bank of the loch, the cold slowly seized me. The wind sounded in my ears under my sou'wester. Wading was not easy: the filling up of the loch after the dams were built had as usual covered up channels and runnels and draining ditches. It is always easy, when wading, stupid with the cold, to step into deep holes. The rain came down in cold grey lines, sometimes half-heartedly, not enough to dimple the water already ruffled by the wind, but at others it fairly whipped and churned the surface. The water, after three hours, soaked through my macintosh. I had tied my handkerchief tightly round my neck to stop it running down my back under my shirt. Nothing moved at all, but I went on casting. At lunch-time I had nothing in my bag, but got into the lee of a green wooden boathouse, ate my sandwiches, drank some whisky and glowed. There was not a soul in sight, nobody else fishing; a few sheep grazed, gulls and curlews called. I saw a few low-swimming, dark cormorants, black and white oyster-catchers with their smart red beaks, a dipper bobbing. The colours of the hills changed every few minutes according to the shading of the clouds, light or dark, and the speed at which they moved. The whole place lowered or shone, though there was not a glimpse of the sun. On the far bank from where I ate, a single red rowan stood out boldly. I had the extraordinary feeling in me that this was my place, no matter how bad the fishing might be.

Late in the afternoon, quite unexpectedly I began to get a few fish. They took very slowly, under water, but they were strong and sporting – though not very big. I remember I got five or six, and when I returned to the hotel like a bedraggled animal at nightfall, dripping and squelching as I walked, I felt, as I laid my catch out on a dish, that Mr Matheson and his household viewed me with a pleased, tolerant astonishment. Was it that only a fool would stay out and fish in such weather? I didn't care. I had a boiling bath, ate my dinner and went to bed, perfectly content.

The remainder of my first stay was cut to the same pattern; days of rain and implacable wind, water inching up as I waded the loch, waders part filled by a wave just topping the thigh, then completely filled by a false step backwards, designed to avoid disaster in front, but leading into some unnoticed hole or drainage channel behind. I caught a few fool fish and was regarded with some awe on this account, and because of the extraordinary amount of water my clothes contained on my return to the hotel in the evenings. At least I established myself as a keen man; and as I see it, people who are completely absorbed by what they are doing, and find solace in what is offered, are most often among the happy and the envied. I think Mr Matheson and his family observed this in me very early and enjoyed my simple pleasure in the fishing and in life at their hotel. I don't know if they knew the first time I stayed there that I was to be a visitor for life. Probably not.

One thing, however, did happen before I left on that first stay which drew my attention to the Truim. The day before I went home it rained twice as hard as on any other day, a cloudburst or, as Mr Matheson called it, a thunder-plump, and for the first time since I had arrived I came in out of the rain. From my bedroom window I looked down into the Truim, suddenly in brown flood. When the rain stopped and the air for a moment became, as it does in the highlands after a storm, sweet and most delicate-smelling, the whole wet world scented because of the wetness, the hills nearer at hand and the sky for a moment clear, I took a line, some lead shot, a hook and a worm and tried the pool near the hotel and two or three down from it. At the third, I hooked and lost what I took to be a very big trout indeed. Opinion in the bar was that it had been a salmon, but I was not sure, and next year, I noted that I must remember, when I returned in the spring, not to neglect the Truim.

5

A DISTRACTING BAY

But by the next year I had forgotten. The Truim, from my bedroom window, still looked rather small and forlorn. It was a cold, sunny, blustery spring with wonderfully vivid colouring on Ericht and in the hills. Donald Grant took me down the loch for the first time, in a boat with an outboard. I was still more interested in the total scene than in the small river.

Donald in a boat is not exactly a communicative person. He takes, apparently, very little notice of you, but in fact watches pretty closely not only you but what you know of nature and of general highland proceedings, whether on the banks of the loch or on the tops of the hills. When he sees, silhouetted 1,500 feet above you on some far skyline, a herd of deer, or an antlered stag, all small as flies, or far away a golden eagle drop suddenly from a crag and, wheeling, ride the air, black against sky or hill on almost motionless wings, he never tells you if you have already seen them yourself.

I soon learnt this. He looked at me sidelong at first from under the peak of his old cap, and when he had ascertained that I was in his and not the city gentleman's world where people must be told about stags and eagles, he said nothing. I do not suppose we spoke a hundred words between the dam at Dalwhinnie and Benalder Cottage twelve miles down the loch, and not more than five hundred the whole day. He took me trolling for Ferox by the Corrivachie inlet tunnel halfway down the loch on the eastern bank – we hooked one fine fish and lost him – and finally came to

Benalder Cottage where we brewed tea and fished first the bay then the far bank of the loch.

We drifted, both fishing, among great rocks, he with one oar in his hand as he fished, seeming to know each stone by name. People say of him that he knew instinctively when a fresh rock of any size rolled down into the loch from a crag. Donald was a lovely fisherman from a boat, fishing with an old, slow, floppy rod very deliberately. He was a great hooker of last-minute fish, when bringing his cast of flies up to the boat. In Ericht the fish are very quick on the take; they follow the flies at a little distance then dart at them in the final second. When he led me by three trout to one, I stopped for a time to watch him; he always kept his eye on the top dropper near the boat, and the moment when it left the water and began to trail and scutter along the tops of the waves was, he said to me, the moment when he expected a fish. I was soon doing the same and have ever since.

When we returned to Dalwhinnie Mr Matheson spoke to me after supper.

'Donald tells me it was one of the best days he ever had on the loch,' he said smiling, apparently very pleased with me.

I was surprised, and said so. We had not caught many fish.

'Donald's a good man and a great man on the loch,' he said: 'and it keeps him off the drink,' he added.

This I could understand, though its dourness could drive you to drink just as easily.

Benalder Cottage, from the day of that first visit with Donald Grant, became one of the distractions which, in my early Dalwhinnie years, kept me from the Truim. It lies in a meadow, very green, on a bay where two small streams flow into the loch. Dominated by Benalder itself, 3,500 feet high, the bay is known as McCook's Bay after a keeper and stalker of that name who lived in the cottage nearly all his life and raised a family in that lonely, beautiful place. Above it is one of the caves in which

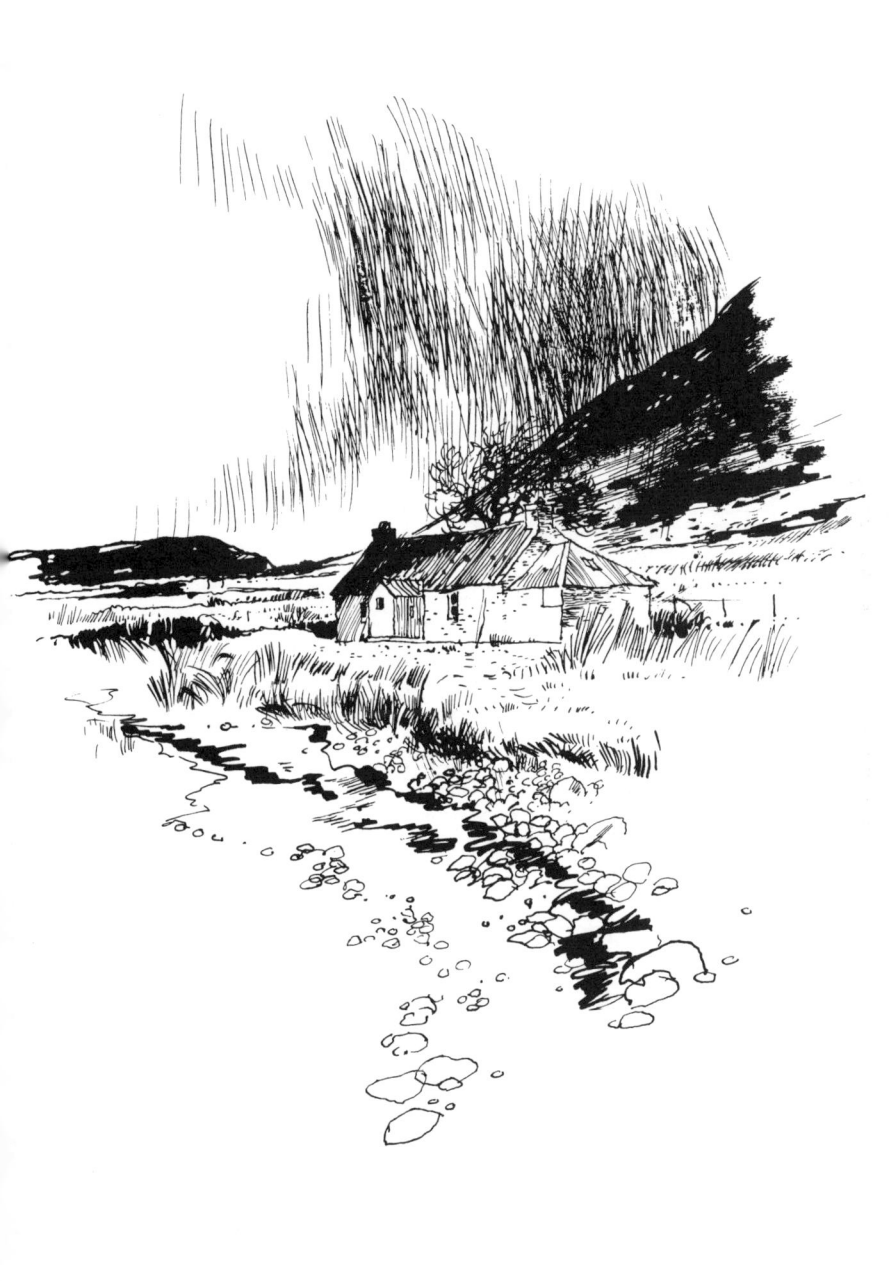

Prince Charlie hid during the flight after his final defeat, but it is said that the cave now visited by walkers and climbers, and named on the map as Prince Charlie's Cave, is in fact not the real cave at all, but one that McCook dug himself with pick and shovel when the true cave became inaccessible to him, as an old man whose legs were failing him. He guided people to the true cave for as many years as he could, for a fee, but in his later days he re-sited it more conveniently in order still to be able to earn from the dead Pretender a part of his living. I would very much like this tale to be true.

For three successive years I went down and stayed for a few days alone at Benalder Cottage, Donald carrying me there by boat, then leaving me. I rarely had company, and to be even for a short time the sole possessor of McCook's Bay, with all that is there – the empty cottage with its good fireplaces, sound slate roof and wooden panelled walls, two rooms and store-room – is to have known the feeling of possessing the whole of beauty and all the kingdoms of this world.

When the sun goes down, the twilight, luminous and rose-coloured, or violet and orange, is long. The bay settles slowly to a peace and a silence that create in the soul such a rapt attention that one walks on tiptoe over the rocks and across the fine green grass, while the wind dies away to a whisper, then to nothing, and the water becomes smooth as oil, only disturbed by an occasional rising fish or the small bow-waves of birds as they swim. On the left lies a long, 500-foot-high rampart of hill with Benalder behind it, stretching towards the open loch. The end of it overlooking the loch has a turret-like flat summit upon which stands a cairn of stones to which each visitor who climbs there adds a stone with his or her name cut on it. There are three stones of mine, waiting there for the last trump.

On the right of the bay is a wood of pines, discreet and orderly, giving the impression of being combed and cultivated, though in fact the falling trees are rarely moved and decay where they fall. Nobody comes to fetch them except the few overnight sleepers at Benalder Cottage who drag them to the wood shed, cut them up, and enjoy thereafter a warm pine-scented, resined sleep as the boughs burn. Opposite the bay lie the hills of the forest of Talla Bheith.

The loneliness and solemn beauty of McCook's Bay have produced an odd social phenomenon in the cottage itself. The walls are inscribed with names and observations, arrowed hearts and pointed wit. There is a splendidly unlikely testimonial to the joys of Benalder attributed to Mr Neville Chamberlain; another to Mahatma Gandhi. The walls are given over to fantasy, delicate observation, serious poetic quotation, nonsense, delighted praise, expressions of sheer contentment, and these invented *obiter dicta* of great men on their imaginary visits. But oddly I could not find a single rude word on one of the walls – and wall-writers, inexplicably, often write rude words – though at one time there was talk of pulling the cottage down on account of the moonshine drinking parties said to be held there. I hope they never do pull it down, since, for perfection, this bay needs its habitation, white, crumbling and grey-roofed, a reminder of the long life of McCook and his family, and of the many who have slept in his rooms since, awed by the bay's solemnity and natural excellence – and by the fishing. For the trout run large at McCook's Bay and on the far bank of the loch opposite to it. The biggest I have had on the fly there is three pounds, and the average is over half a pound.

Anyway, whether it was the trout or the scene, for three years McCook's kept me from any save the most cursory visits to the Truim; and I don't regret it.

FIRST TRUE DAY

So it was not until my fourth year at Dalwhinnie that I attacked the Truim seriously. By seriously, I mean giving the river a whole day. I did it for the worst of reasons; because the wind and the cold on Loch Ericht had been such that for two days not a fish had moved. You could cast from morning until night and you got no touch; and all day long the hard wind blew until your fingers crooked and froze as you struggled with wind-snags in your cast or removed hooks from your ears or from the back of your coat – from that precise point which you cannot reach without undressing. There was no sense in it. The sky was leaden and the clouds had no light in them, so the colours of the hills were painted over by a daylong mist of greyness.

The morning on which I began started wet; a steady thin downpour, not the kind that rings on the window-panes, but the kind that soaks rather than beats through every known coat and jacket except an oilskin, which is too hot to fish in all day.

After breakfast Mr Matheson said, according to his now established formula:

'Well, what's the programme for today?'

I said I thought I'd try the Truim.

FIRST TRUE DAY

'Anyway it can't be worse than the loch,' he said.

There is never any unhealthy enthusiasm from anyone for the fishing at Dalwhinnie when the weather is unfavourable. Nor in fact will any truly knowing person readily commit himself about it when the weather is good. That which is insecure and uncertain is accepted as insecure and uncertain without unnecessary fuss, remembering that at Dalwhinnie, even at the best of the season, you never can tell. So I took my sandwiches, filled my whisky flask and was driven up the main road north to the small side turning that leads to Loch Cuaich, halfway between Dalwhinnie and Crubenmore Bridge. This is the most exposed stretch of the river, the upper two miles. I got out of the car into half a gale. The wind had risen since before breakfast, and the rain was harder; no longer the soft downpour of the early morning. The river flows at this point quite near the road; a lane leads to it and the river was spanned by a rickety wooden bridge which has since been replaced by an inelegant, safe, sober concrete one; the lane then crosses the railway line to a group of keepers' cottages and eventually leads up the hill to Loch Cuaich. Mr Matheson waved me his usual cheerful, slightly incredulous, gallows farewell and drove off. I paddled through the wet grass and along the wet road, still confident and breakfast-warm, to the river.

On my first morning, I knew nothing of the Truim, its water, flies or manners. I tied with wet, shiny, chilling fingers, three wet flies to a cast – it was late May and I chose a Butcher at point, an Olive for bob, and a Blue and Black at top dropper. All this time I stood back to the wind as anyone in his senses would, but I knew by the feel of the rain on my back that I was to spend the whole day wet through. Though my sou'wester protected my neck, I knew this couldn't last, so as usual I tied a handkerchief round my throat before I began to fish.

When I did, I started with orthodoxy, the wind on my back, downstream, like every other Scot, like everyone not prepared to push a dry fly into half a gale all day long, and swear and swear and swear when it never reaches a single point he aims at. I only stood well back and let rod and line work for me, using the wind as a licensed carrier, and letting the line fall mostly on the river bank with only the cast in the water.

Even in the worst conditions, there is a beguiling magic to the first minutes of a day trout-fishing. I look around me and feel an independent man, within harm's reach and not inviolable, but with my thoughts limited and enlarged by the narrow compass of my eyes. My vision extends backward into time and forward into time, and I remember for a moment fishers past, and that I shall grow too old for it in the end and that others will follow me, and that this small piece of river will change hardly at all in a thousand years. My function of intellecting and adorning the world is particularly dear to me beside a river, and I am willing for it to be the master, if the master is necessarily the more durable of two things, which is arguable. At least we fail to outlive one of our suits of clothes, one pair of our boots, and fishers, some of their fishing-rods. This is why it is a joyful thing for me that I sometimes fish with one of my father's trout rods that I inherited from him after he was killed in the First World War in 1916. Because of this, I can think of him still as taking part.

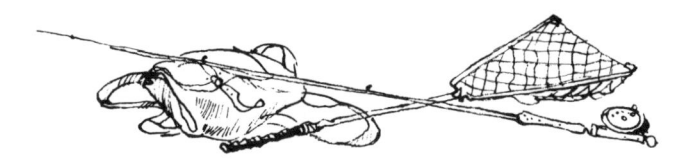

Below the Cuaich Bridge there is quite a swift little run. Beyond it to the right is the burn that flows down the hill from Loch Cuaich, almost dry save in flood-time ever since Cuaich was dammed as part of the North of Scotland hydro-electric scheme. There is a pool that the burn dug in the Truim bed, then the river turns a quarter left and runs towards the road. Beside the road lies a big, deep pool, a holding pool where those salmon rest that come up from the Spey and have had the luck and the guile to escape local poachers who are skilful, thorough and exceptionally observant about salmon, as all decent, secretive salmon-eating countrymen should be.

From the Cuaich Bridge, I took the right bank of the stream, over the bed of Cuaich burn, covering the river with erratic wind-borne casts as I went. In spite of the cold, one or two fish rose. I took them to be small ones. They plucked at the fly quickly as trout always seem to when they come short in cold weather and high wind; in fact it is generally an error on the part of the fisher. Right at the tail of the burn pool, suddenly I hooked a lively half-pounder. He came up, yellow and glistening, took the fly and was taken by me in under a minute, a nice fat short fish with a big broad tail. Twenty paces farther on, in a very narrow run on the far bank I had another, a little smaller but still of a size to be kept. Both had taken Olives, so I took off my Blue and Black from the top dropper position and put on a female March Brown, switched my Olive from bob to point, and my Butcher to bob.

FISHING A HIGHLAND STREAM

While I was doing this the rain came down so hard that the surface of the water hissed and bubbled; I could feel it penetrating my clothes; it ran down my face and I could almost watch the pads of pink flesh on the ends of my fingers wrinkle. Then as suddenly the rain stopped; a thin, skilly beam of sun shone for half a minute, then blinked in as if discouraged by its own daring. I dried and polished my glasses with the dry cloth I always keep hidden in a polythene bag in my innermost pocket, then walked clattering over the smooth stones towards the pool by the road which, on the far side from where I was, is walled by a beautiful outcrop of warm, red rock.

The wind still blew a gale; the cold was piercing, real whisky weather. You had to keep casting to keep warm, fish or no fish. But at this pool, as it turned out, it was to be fish; one fish. Standing well away from the bank I put out fifteen yards of line so that most of it lay on the stones at my feet, between me and the water. I watched the cast hiss through the air and roll out neatly, covering the deep flow of the pool where the head of the run swirled and twisted, and seconds later the backwater over the sandbank on my side of the river. It was just as the cast of flies moved from the current to the backwater that a big trout rolled up, very leisurely, as fish do on warm, southern chalk streams, on soft golden days, and I could almost watch my bob fly into his mouth. I tightened and he ran down the stream like a rocket, me following, taking in line as I ran. Twenty-five yards away, there is a swift stickle with rocks, leading to the outlet of the pool, and bearing the main, strong current. I had to keep the fish in the pool or risk losing him, so I stopped, bent my rod on him with side-strain until he halted and shook his head; then he suddenly jumped and ran upstream. It was a joy to see him leap, glistening and shimmering in the air. I lowered the head of my rod, took the strain again, then ran noisily into the pool, splashing deliberately to show my presence.

Though the rain poured on and almost blinded me by soaking my glasses, I managed to keep my fish in sight. He ran swiftly up and down, guided by me, coming closer to the bank with every run. I began to wrestle with my collapsible landing net which as usual had tied itself in an inextricable knot. It took me three minutes and my favourite oaths to unravel it in time to take that large, most patient, well-hooked trout. It made its last hard run on seeing me and realizing the nature of its danger, then came in rolling, on its side; I slipped the net under it and a moment later had my first Truim two-pounder on the stones. It was two pounds three ounces in fact, a brilliantly coloured fish, red spotted with a golden-pink sheen to its skin, which is a peculiarity of Truim and Spey trout in May and June, as I afterwards discovered.

For the rest of the day, for nine solitary hours, I saw nothing more, felt no touch. The Truim as though shocked by its burst of generosity had utterly closed down. The cold, I suppose, was too intense. I fished in a trance most of the time, moving about for warmth. When I sat down behind a stone above the Quarry pool to have lunch I took my pretty fish from the bag and admired him like a miser who carries in his pocket the last gold nugget in the world.

It was this fish and this stormy May day, containing in its long ten hours perhaps a quarter of an hour of sport, that turned my attention finally away from Ericht, my first Dalwhinnie affection, to the Truim. Now I love them both; they are a beautiful though damned unladylike pair.

THE APPROACH

A portrait is generally a thing of talent, the adroitness, the prejudices of the painter, a mirror of the disrespect or excess of respect he feels for his subject. What spoils a portrait for one makes it for another, and for two people speaking of the same portrait, lifelike can be a dirty word or high praise. To portray with personal delicacy and discrimination, 'warts and all', may be the honourable course.

This picture of the Truim is intended to be such a portrayal, but must also come near to being a betrayal, in which I shall be revealed as much as my river. In such circumstances it may be a defect to love; one excuses too easily, one rhapsodizes, when a denunciation might, on merit, be a better award. Yet, even if I denounced the Truim, enchantment would still break through; it would be out of character, so I had best not try it.

The chapters which follow will be a picture of the physical habit, the life, the feed, the fish, the flowers, the stones, the spring face, the air that surrounds, the whole circumstance and public appearance, complete with winds, noises off, attendant people, dogs, sheep, deer and rabbits, of the Truim; and also how to fish it. It has been amassed and stored by my brain now for six or seven years, and I think I know the river only a little less well than the back of my hand or the lumps and contours of my face in the shaving mirror of a morning.

It quickens me, when I am far away, to think of it. I am absurdly fascinated by it. It beckons and consoles. I greet it every year from my sleeper window, with heart-quickening excitement, as I go over the Pass of Drumochtar in the train. I see the early sun glint on its first narrow pools and am at peace and at home. This river portrait should reveal the Truim's intimate anatomy, which has a bearing on that of the many dozens of small rivers like it. The same will be true of the descriptions of how to fish it which I shall intertwine with the narrative.

I shall start at that point about three-quarters of a mile below the Laggan Bridge, where the lady vanishes and becomes part of the Spey. No lady ever vanished or was absorbed in the stream of history more elegantly and creditably.

But before I begin, what are the data? What are the essential decisions which I have taken about the Truim, about the Scots burn, as to the manner of fishing it? This is necessary, for the whole procedure of description will be based on these decisions.

First, for my money, the shimmering clear, swift-running burn can and should be fished with a dry fly, upstream. It is a technique that has to be learned when the river flows fast, as does the Truim. But since I have done it successfully now on many other burns and rivers which are not famous for the size of their fish, and have so regularly turned up with one or two fish at least twice the often arbitrarily decreed 'normal' size for the water, I can only believe that the best, wariest, largest fish in many burns are never seen by most fishers, and rarely caught. Many fishers are spotted by the trout, when approaching the river with little, if any, intelligent precaution, often with the sun behind them, often making no attempt to use natural cover, or even without stooping to avoid casting a shadow on the water. Downstream burn fishing for trout can certainly be done – by standing well back from the water's edge so that the line after casting often lies on the land, and little more than the cast falls on the water. But upstream dry fly is by far the best on burns as on chalk streams.

Upstream wet fly, too, can be excellent, though not quite as satisfying aesthetically as dry.

Secondly, if you accept upstream dry fly as the most effective method of burn fishing, to wade is almost essential, for two reasons – convenience, for getting into position to cover a rising fish, and for control of the fish once hooked. A large part of success in hooking and landing a good trout in rough water and narrow, treed streams lies in not letting it get below and behind one: consequently the moment I hook a good fish in such a stream I splash hard, make a disturbance, and am noisy. The fish rarely makes a dash past me, and it is kept going upstream or from side to side by the knowledge that there is an obstacle to a downstream run; it tires more quickly and its evolutions are less dangerous, though often spectacular.

Thirdly, it means a particular kind of rod, notably for the Truim where the winds are very strong indeed, and when one faces upstream, almost invariably headwinds. The rod should be about nine feet, quite stiff and with a lot of drive from the butt; the line should be double-tapered silk, dressed, the cast nylon three X or two X according to the weight of water and the time of day. I have experimented for some time with nylon casts, however, and have found that a good caster can land his fly very lightly indeed with stouter nylon than would be possible with gut. On the Truim, which flows fast, though it is extremely clear, I can use two X in rough water even on sunny days and get no diminution in the number of rises.

Fourthly, it is essential in a cold river where the rise is often very sparse and sometimes non-existent accurately to 'read the river' as I call it, which means to divine as one approaches the likely spots where good fish are likely to lie, and in what order to fish them.

Fifthly and finally, in a very clear stream, one must suit the cadence of one's movement to the force of the wind. On a still day

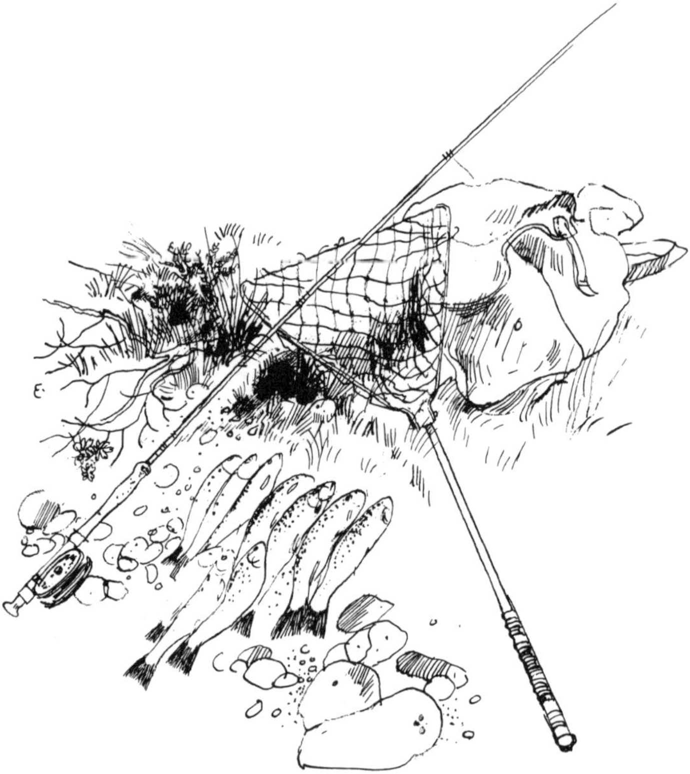

one must walk and gesture more slowly than on a day when the whole orchestra is playing, because trees, bushes, heather, grass, reeds all stand still, and one's movement is thus more visible. In a high wind, within reason, and among trees, one can afford to move fast, jerkily, or even, on occasion, carelessly.

These then are my small lists of assumptions for successful burn fishing; now to apply them to my physical portrait of the Truim.

The Spey above and below where the Truim joins it is a noble, though diminished river. It has not any longer the grandeur and rolling solemnity of its famous beats, but it is still a broad, fast river, smooth-surfaced, with long runs and great pools, and when you wade in it, the pull of the current on your legs has an authority that the Truim lacks. It contains some magnificent trout, which rise particularly well during the season of the hatching of the Olive in May and June. I once had, just below the Truim confluence, four trout between two and two and a half pounds each from a single long, swift, broken-water run, in an hour of a late May morning. On the Spey during Olive time, wise men watch the flight of the swifts and swallows. No matter how high the wind, if you see the swallows come down and skim the water, you know exactly what they are picking up, and generally in a few minutes, however cold the air, the rise begins. The difficulty about the Spey at such times is the sheer brutality of the wind. The water below the Truim is so exposed that when there is a high wind very often you cannot get your fly out at all; in which case you must either leave the rising fish or take a chance fishing downstream and perhaps moving one in ten.

The Truim joins the Spey at an angle of about 45 degrees from the Spey's course. The confluence is at the end of a typical long, deep Spey pool containing a lot of mixed weed. In it I have seen some very large trout indeed, but never caught one, not because they are not risers and takers, but because in all the time I have known the place, the wind conditions have never been favourable for fishing it effectively on the days when I have been there. This is very typical of short, annual holidays in stormy places; fishing favourite spots may elude you for seasons at a time.

But it is good to stand at the point of juncture and look, from the broad bed of big smooth stones on Truim's left bank, up to Creige Duibbe Lodge set on its green hill, the fine river in the foreground. The main current of the Spey is on the far bank here, so the Truim water flows right across the width of the Spey and joins it there. It has dug its own shallow trough in the big river's bed, and to fish it you must wade straight up the Truim current, fanning out your casts in front of you, particularly in the centre of the stream and along the backwater of the deep Spey pool to the right. Short casts all along the edge of this deep water sometimes get fine fish, but when the sun is warm they are more usually in the centre; and the bigger the fish, the more quietly they take – a pensive surface dimple, a small movement; you see it sometimes only out of the corner of your eye – and a natural fly vanishes. These are the ones to beware of because here you can break in a fish that will give you the shock of your life. But the wind will only allow you to fish this spot properly perhaps once in ten days. Here, last year, a gift of the wind, I collected an Olive ear ring, piratically, hooked straight through the left lobe, which I cut out with a razor blade only when I got back to Dalwhinnie eight hours later.

To get to the place where the Truim joins the Spey, I am dropped by car at Etteridge where there is a signal box and a small siding. I cross the railway bridge with the two quietly smoking cottages beside it and step over a taut wire fence into a lightly treed meadow, thick with moss. I hurry a little down the steep slope towards the river, spurred by that small maniac fisherman's feeling that the river may get away, be suddenly drained at a gulp by some Spey drought, or be fished to death by miscreants in the ten minutes before I can get to it. Whatever the reason, I hurry, putting up a hare or a rabbit perhaps, and watching it white-tail away at speed. Curlews call and tumble as they fly. There are black-faced hill sheep, long-woolled, with lambs at foot. I am a talented sheep linguist and exchange baas with numbers of what I view, quite wrongly, as old friends, as I go by. It seems to give pleasure to all.

At the bottom of the treed slope lies a small bog in which roots and branches of dead trees lie half-buried, or sometimes on the surface, dried by the wind or wet with rain, but all hardened by time. They are like groups or single pieces of modern sculpture, weird, expressive, forceful, incomplete, pierced with holes, tortured yet with familiarity and appeal. Each year I take, on the four or five occasions when I visit the Spey–Truim confluence, different routes across the bog to see the different pieces with which I have grown familiar. Some of them are now well known

FISHING A HIGHLAND STREAM

to me; it is like visiting the garden of a careless collector, or taking a stroll on a more mysterious Easter Island.

You can see the river, small and shining, from the top of the slope, and just across it, backed by hills, is a keeper's cottage, white and excellently lonely, where lives a shrill, attentive dog tied to a kennel. It is a perennial game and one of the pleasures of memory to expect the bark of that dog to begin as I come down the hill or across the bog, particularly on the first visit of the year. I attach an absurd importance to not being spotted and barked at too soon, for I have declared secretly to myself that the best fishing is to be had on the days when he sees me latest. My record day, some years ago, was when he did not see me at all and I went past in tense silence, waiting for his excited yelps and barks as for a revelation or the expected solo in an anthem. None came.

After the bog, there is a broad, green, undulating, cropped sheep field, very springy underfoot, with the ruins of a stone house lying between the bog and the river, a primitive outline drawn in fallen stone of a living room, a bedroom and a sheep-fold. There is a round machine-gun post too, soon to be as ancient, unbelievable and legendary as a Roman encampment, but recalling the days when highlanders were sometimes heard to observe that if Hitler happened to beat the British and invaded Scotland, it would be a long war.

I describe these things because they are for me part of the deep satisfaction of trout fishing, and to see them again after a many-month-long interval quickens my heart; or when I am not there, stirs my memory. It is a very different kind of company from city company and the din of traffic, to greet sheep and birds and ruined houses and shrill, small dogs, in an air that is infinitely fresh and pure, even when cold and wet.

So let it now be considered that I have been dog-spotted and barked at; that the curlews have called mournfully, the sheep have been conversed with solemnly; and that I am at the mouth of the Truim, past the Spey entry pool, and wading upstream.

8

THE FINE-SPUN PORTRAIT I

I shall speak of it as a late spring stream. Almost the only trout you will get in April on the Truim will be on the worm during a flood, but even that is very uncertain. Put your hand in Truim water in April and you will know why; it is piercingly cold. None of the wet flies, the March Brown, the Butcher, the Greenwell, the Blue and Black, the Teal and Green will provoke a single rise. The water looks quite without life, and you can walk the length of it without spotting a movement.

But in May it changes. In the backwaters under trees particularly, and in at the bank, you begin to see the Little Iron Blue, that distinctive, tiny, essentially cold-weather fly. On days when they take it, fishing is quite easy, but it is rarely the main taking fly all day on the Truim. The thing to watch for is the start of the Olive hatch, which generally happens around the 15th of May or a little later. The Sooty Olive and the Rough Olive usually turn up a few days earlier, in smallish numbers, then comes the Olive proper. They continue all through the second half of May and most of June and bring on the best fishing of the year, if good fishing there is to be, which is not always the case. In June and early July are added the Tupp and the Black Gnat, then in mid-July the Alder. But by mid-July, let it be said, the 'good' fishing on the Truim is pretty well over for the year, except for a short St Martin's summer in September, if the weather holds.

In late July and August you will wonder as much where the water has gone as where the fish have gone. The pools often grow stagnant with only a trickle flowing through them; the water itself is very clear, but tired and whisky brown; a few rings of dirty foam float apathetically downstream. Nothing ever happens, and only rarely by waiting beside a deep still pool do you see even the shadow of a trout. The only thing to do in August is to go out with a fine cast and some pale Duns towards evening when the air grows russet as the sun sinks and reddens, and watch for a rise among the deep, still black pools at the Falls of Truim. In the quiet hours before nightfall you may get perhaps one good fish.

I have given you the main flies for which you will be looking on the Truim water as you face upstream. Only two further warnings; first, on the Truim if a good and apparently taking fish repeatedly lets a fly of the species that is on the water pass him, particularly an Olive, take it off and try a small black sunken

Nymph; secondly, hook sizes should invariably be small; the flies are very hard to see on the rough water, but it is always better to fish too small than too large on the Truim.

As with all burns and quickly flowing rivers, the flow of the Truim is deceptive. It gives the impression of being rougher and shallower than it is, like many people. View it from a high bank and you think that for long stretches it is hardly worth fishing. View it wading upstream, from the level of the water itself, and you see that though seemingly broken and turbulent, the river often makes for itself a long regular series of graduated steps, in which the water, perpetually flowing, has dug often quite deep small pools where fish can congregate or one large fish lie, feed well and grow fat. So one should never be deceived on a burn by an impression that a long stickle or turbulent run is in fact a single piece of level water, running over a level bed, or too shallow to hold a good fish. You can prove this when you walk up the Truim in spring; many good fish run out from right under your feet from behind quite small stones that are half buried in the river bed, and round which the flow of the water has removed sand and gravel and made a hole, the existence of which you could only guess at as you approached it. So as I wade, I set a fly two feet above every single sizeable stone to which I can force it. A couple of casts; no more – unless I have seen a rise, in which case I give it half a dozen.

The first run of the Truim is just such a place as I have described. You wade up with the water mostly only to your ankles, but sometimes to your knees, searching the small step-pools with a couple of casts near the stones. A big stone in the pool with an oak tree beside it on the far bank is my favourite place there, but only for reasons of obstinacy. I never rose a fish by that stone in my life, but it is a natural place for a trout to lie, and therefore every year I waste minutes on it, insisting un-reasonably, and excusing my failure by saying to myself as I leave that I may have been forestalled by some earlier phantom fisher – a likely tale! But perhaps I would wait there anyway; the window-clattering ruin of a blue-slated stone cottage stands near by, and for some reason I like to give its walls a small sight of life, and make a place where people once breathed and bred again briefly inhabited. Also, on the oak tree there is often to be seen a small brown owl, roosting sleepily. I see him almost every year and declare him, against all the odds, to be the identical, unchanging permanent duty owl on guard at the mouth of the Truim and over that fallen cottage.

After this first run, there is a long stickle, very shallow except near the top, in which I have never caught a fish. The river then turns first sharp right, then sharp left and there is a treed-up smooth run fifteen yards long where, if the wind is favourable – which is almost never – and you can reach them among the branches, good fish lie under the bank among the tree-roots that make it overhang a little where the water has washed the earth away. Then comes the first good pool of the river, into which a tree fell a few years ago, utterly spoiling it. The big branches dug into the gravel and the pool quickly silted up. In a few years' time – or perhaps this season even – the dead tree will shift suddenly in some flood, the pool will hollow out again, and trout will return. The natural changes in a river's face from year to year always give pleasure.

Thirty yards further on, starting on a right-handed corner, is the longest and best pool in the lower reaches of the Truim. It merits detailed description because it can, on occasion, hold so many good fish that I have come to regard it as my touchstone for the day's fishing. It is also a pool of classic stamp, shallow near the outflow, with sallies all up the right bank where the water is deepest, and a clear left bank with pale grey stones bordered by green cropped grass. Large rounded boulders lie in it, some entirely covered by the water, others showing. The water deepens quite quickly after the outflow, and soon reaches almost to the top of thigh waders. The pool itself is about fifty yards long, smooth-surfaced for about thirty yards, and in the sun you can watch the whole fly-taking process when you have spotted a fish, because it is very clear and the fish run quite large, though they rise with extreme tact and gentleness, barely dimpling the surface. Unwary fishers easily break in a trout here. As on land, so in water. The really big ones do not make much of a splash. They think it vulgar or unwise.

On this pool you will not get a single fish if you wade carelessly and let waves precede you up the current from the smooth lower water.

A few years ago I met a Polish Scot or a Scottish Pole from the wartime immigration fishing here and getting nothing, only because he was a clumsy wader. He was a big man and fished well but roughly, trained probably by the violence of the Scottish winds to press, and insist on the fly hissing out at all costs. He stamped about in the water like an amphibious, legged tank, purposefully but very noisily. After we had smoked together for half an hour in the lee of a bank, resting, out of the wind, I went and took two trout from where he had just been fishing. He watched me smiling and with a decent grace in spite of the insult, then summed the matter up in a memorably peculiar phrase:

'Ah! I, too much splash! Must make rehashmentation method of walking in water? Yes.'

He winked as he spoke, and, a huge man, demonstrated by tiptoeing absurdly along the grass in mightily exaggerated silence how quiet he must now be. I never saw him again, but I am prepared to bet that he got more fish after this incident. It is an illusion that one can with impunity wade clumsily and splash in swift-flowing water merely because nature is a little noisy.

The trouble about this run is the old one, the one that constantly recurs and will recur in this book, the wind. Eight

THE FINE-SPUN PORTRAIT I

times out of ten, the wind conspires either to blow your cast straight back in your face or into the attendant line of sallies. The only answer is to keep the fly low when false-casting, and thrust it hard into the eye of the wind angled at least 30 degrees away from the spot where you want to set it. By doing this you will get over your rise one cast in ten, if you are lucky. The rest are just Truim exercise. For on this baleful little river you have to count on using very few of the casts you actually make. It is why I recommend a light and powerful rod; above all light.

Now the river continues.

It turns to the left at the top of the run in a smooth arc. On this turn I fish only at one point, where a big smooth stone sits, well into the bank of the river. Around it, save at its very base, the water is shallow. Once, five years ago, in June, when the river was on the rise after rain, I came on a salmon behind that stone, resting before a move upstream, and walked to within a yard of it. For this wholly insufficient reason I always expect to find a large trout there, but never do. The senseless and the unreasonable, in fishing as in much else, are infinitely attractive to me. I watch my life being corrupted by superstition as I fish; I will insist, for example, on sitting on a particular stone for lunch by a pool, because once, years back, I caught a fine trout after sitting on that stone for lunch. Or when the fish are not rising I recite long, sonorous pieces of poetry to them in a loud voice, bellowing into the wind. There is nothing that bores trout so completely – Herder, Milton, Spenser and Victor Hugo are the best – and they become quite distracted, yawn, and so make, for them, the fatal mistake. This method is also recommended for dour Scottish lochs when boat fishing; though one may recall, perhaps, that recitation also serves to keep oneself awake when, for hour after hour, one casts and casts with no response. It means that when a trout comes, at least one is at home to greet it.

But to return to my stone, after it for a hundred yards the

water is of little use; too shallow. So I walk on the green grass bank, and here am spotted again by the chained dog at the keeper's cottage which lies, as I have said, lonely, on the far shore and is first seen as one comes down from Etteridge. I fish the whole of the next stretch to the new, refreshing sound of barks, shrill and excited; it is something to which one grows accustomed and for which one waits and would miss. A fallen tree in the main stream is the next landmark; the white skeleton of a sheep lies behind it, that I have known through all its seasons of corruption from the day it died lambing five years ago. I slip into the water just upstream of this tree where the current is strong and the water deep, having dried my line beforehand, and fish standing right in the stream, sitting my fly down for seconds on every patch of unbroken but swirling water; three years ago I had a good fish there, none since. Filed away in the memory, small past incidents dictate the pattern of the new days.

Above this point the river, after a short run, turns sharply to the right. I cross over – this is an excellent place to fill one's waders, for one is tempted to inch across among the slippery rocks in a place which is really much too deep – and try the tail of the run on the corner. It is normally almost impossible to fish for two reasons, the wind and the fact that the swift stream carries your line down the current and there is drag on the fly after a few seconds. One year in three there is a chance of a fish at this spot, and it is often a good one; but you are also tantalized by seeing good trout roll there on the many more impossible days.

After the turning, a tree which the current is gradually uprooting – I have watched the process over the years – overhangs the water. It is at the outflow of a neat, pretty little stickle, with a grass bank upstream from the tree where the water is deep; then a clump of flags and five yards of sprouting sallies.

The thing to do here is to fish one's own bank first – though this will nearly always be dead into the wind – then put out twice as much line as one needs, shoot it upstream and let the wind blow it right over to the far bank so that the fly runs down the stream a few inches from the edge. At first, one loses a few flies doing this, but in time one grows cunning. This sally hedge, fish apart, is a particular enchantment because it always seems to be full of wrens bobbing about, brown, tiny, and somehow aggressive, from twig to twig. I invariably greet them as I go by, probably scaring them stiff, though I believe them to be the most savage of birds.

Beyond the stickle lies a long deep pool dotted with big smooth stones, with trees on either side of it. It is only when their thin screen to the right of you as you wade has hidden you that the dog stops barking and, slightly surprised, you find yourself in silence, or among new sounds. There is generally a pair of dippers on this pool; they move ahead of you from rock to rock, bobbing and bowing like slightly agitated courtiers before too large a king.

This pool, though surely inhabited, rarely yields a trout. I fish it carefully the first time I go up it, every year, then neglect it, giving it a few casts near the head as I pass on other days. It is one of the spots which should be excellent and are not; pretty, ordered, tidy, sheltered and exactly the right depth, it tantalizes, enchants and refuses to yield.

Not so the next stretch; difficult, narrow, treed and requiring the utmost accuracy and cunning, the trout are there if you can get them. Lined on the right bank with sally and birch, overhanging the water, the wind is practically always on your quarter as you fish; it is an exposed stretch from there to the Laggan Bridge, so the wind hits harder. It is also a place which, owing to its difficulty, causes me to concentrate fiercely and neglect my wading. I have twice slipped on stones here and fallen backwards into the water, filling waders, soaking myself to the skin, waterlogging sandwiches, and bringing me every other special blessing accorded to the fallen. But it is no less a fascinating place.

At the beginning, the trees overhang the water and the trout rise right under them. After fishing your own bank – the water is two or three feet deep – you cast, wind or no wind, straight at the trees, checking, pulling, tweaking, using the wind as a carrier or fighting against it, to sit your fly just where the leaves of the trees trail in the water. Your line is rarely taut, so you do not touch more than one rise in three.

The pool, remaining narrow and small, then deepens and is turbulent; the wind whips it and you rarely see your fly because of this and the shadows from the bank, but there is always one fine trout there, if you can get it. Just above the pool lies a big rock, round which the water humps and swirls, but I have never found a way to extract a fish here intentionally. I have tried collapsing my line into the pool behind it, so that the fly and cast sit for a second to the right or left of the rock, but nothing happens. Once and once only, in high wind and rain, after lashing about furiously for two minutes like an angry coachman with a whip, I suddenly saw my fly for a reason which I have never been able to explain, sitting demurely beside the rock, on the water, defying gravity and the stream, and being taken a second later by a trout of over a pound which I afterwards netted in the pool below.

Beyond the rock is another small sally-lined run, just like the first, which always contains fish. A birch tree has fallen across it at the head, and the best trout lie at the precise spot which guarantees that before you leave the run you hook up in the tree. They, too, feed where the branches trail in the water. So the time you spend at this pool has a term set to it by the tree.

Above the tree is a stretch of fifty yards of broken water up the middle of which you should wade, fishing the 'steps' that I have described to you. The way to do it is to flip out your line, about three yards more than you need, then let the wind blow the cast back towards you as you set the fly down, at the same time pulling back sharply the spare line with your free hand. The result, which probably defies all the laws of mechanics, is that the fly sits on the object 'step' pool, the cast crumpled around it, while the line lies in the 'step' below. Here it is pulled away more slowly by the current, and in consequence the fly on the step 'stays put' for a few seconds more than it would have; this gets you fish.

Everybody fishes pools and runs and stickles; they are visible and obvious places. I take a special delight, on rivers like the Truim, in taking often the best fish of the day from broken water such as this.

By now, you can see the elegant stone Laggan Bridge that crosses the water at Etteridge. You can see too the fine round pool below it, the little copse to the right of it, and the smooth-water

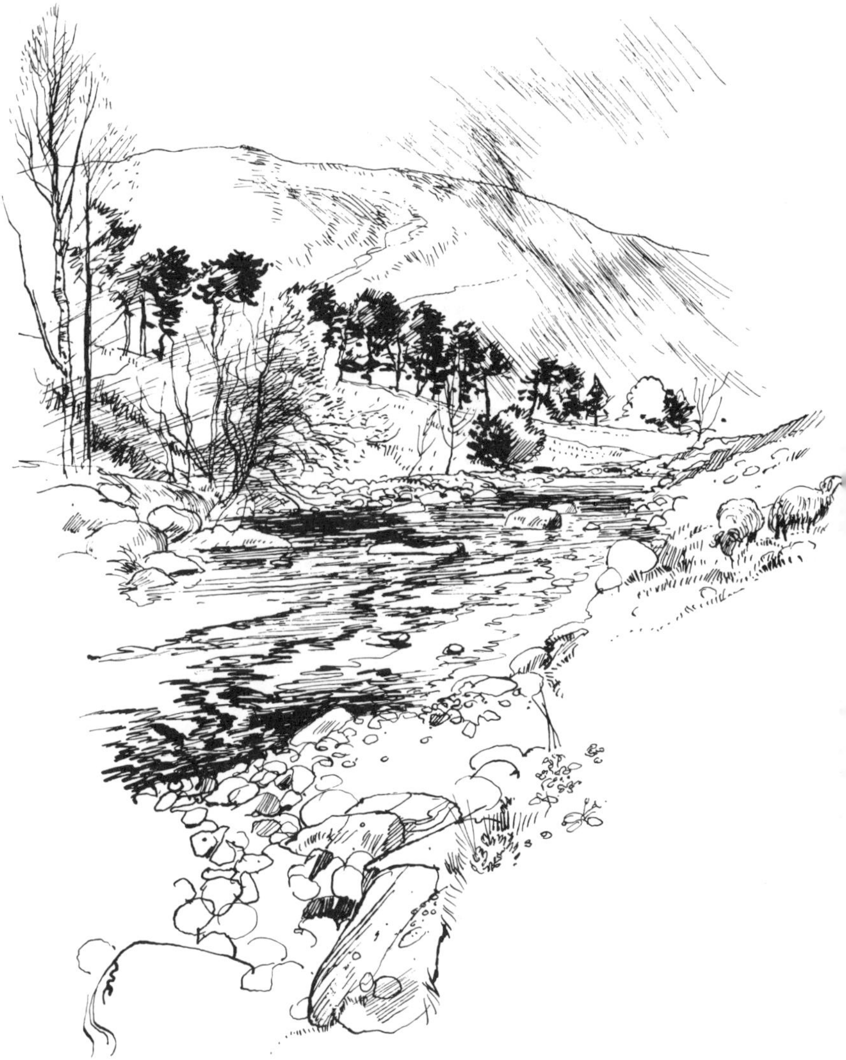

approach to the pool. The left bank there is green and almost clear of trees and in spring is always rich in sheep and lambs with whom I have my usual baa-discussions as I move up the water. I often wonder what magical compliments I pay them which make the old sheep breathe more rapidly and the young lambs laugh and skip.

This pool below Laggan Bridge is a place to pause and have lunch. One should lie back on the grass bank with one's head on a chosen rock for comfort, and watch what is going on in the pool, for there is always a lot going on. I have a special stone there with, for me, long-standing magical properties

THE FINE-SPUN PORTRAIT II

Lying back watching the Laggan pool as I have lunch, I take care to put my rod down out of arm's reach. It is a lesson in self-control to say to oneself:

'The big trout lying above that rock will go on feeding for the next half-hour; watch him and think how you can catch him.'

Obviously, sometimes one has been weak and fished sandwich in hand, or with mouth stuffed full of bread. I hardly do it at all now, because I know this Laggan pool. The fish really will wait. Besides which some laziness is, I believe, medically a duty when one is over forty.

The pool is pleasantly noisy, for the sound of the water echoes under the arches of the bridge. The main flow is through the centre arch over a deeply indented lip of the dark rock to which the bridge is anchored. To the left, three yards below the overflow, protruding from the water, stands a large rounded stone, a perfect shelter for trout. Beyond it, just upstream to the left, there is a rocky shelf above which the water is rarely more than a foot deep. The current sweeps first along this shelf, turns back to form a backwater, then joins the main stream above the stone at an angle to the right. The whole of the right-hand side of the pool is also a backwater, except when the river is in spate and water also flows through the second arch of the bridge.

I lie as I eat, fifteen yards below the bridge, right at the outflow of the pool, which is probably four feet deep at its deepest point under the fall when the flow of the river is normal. The rock at the bottom of the pool is chrome yellow, and in the clear water

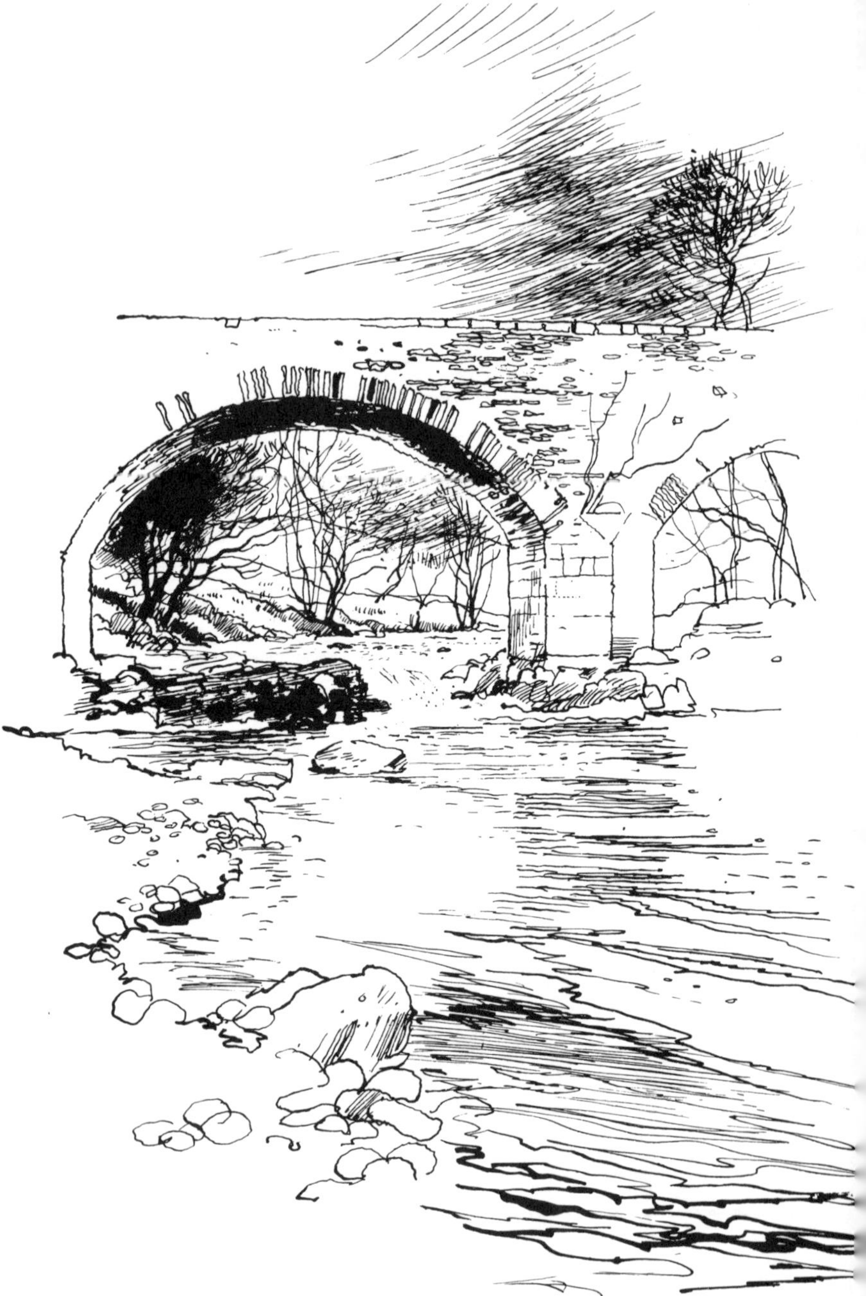

you can see small trout moving about and feeding, but it is only rarely that a good fish comes down to the lower end of the pool. They remain mostly about a yard above the big stone and slightly to the right of it. It is perfectly easy to cast the fly to where they are, but it only sits without drag for about three seconds because the current below the rock on which your floating line lies is pulling straight downstream, whereas the current above the stone is angled to the right.

The thing to do, therefore, is to spot to within six square inches the points at which good fish are rising and land your fly not more than a foot above them. If you are inaccurate, you won't get fish, and on most days the odds are strongly against your being accurate owing to the wind. I get from this pool perhaps two good trout in ten days of fishing, or five visits to the pool. The rest of the time I am blown from the water, swearing, and the trout remain behind.

There is a fine echo under the bridge and as I pass through it I have formed the habit of having a good yell. It clears the lungs, is a pleasantly brainless action, and some answer to the incessant bird-song. To the left at the other side of the bridge is the remains of the vegetable garden of a vanished house – early wild raspberries grow there for the eating – and after one of these yells a startled sheep is often to be found standing bewildered in the long grass, wondering presumably why I, who normally baa so comprehensibly at sheep as the whole neighbourhood knows, should suddenly produce so unsheeplike a noise.

Above the bridge, for a hundred yards or so, the river is, for the Truim, quite wide, and flows swiftly down a relatively steep gradient. The bed is scattered with large rocks, and very slippery underfoot. All the way up, if you wade from side to side, there are the small, hidden underwater pools of which I have spoken, and where good trout often lie. The banks here are thickly treed, but there is room to cast if you keep to the centre of the stream, fishing right and left as you move. Here I catch trout when the sun is brilliant; for the water glitters and is shade-dappled. You stand still for a minute and watch for natural flies among the stones, find a place where there is a hatch coming down, and put your fly among them, remembering that in rough water it is easier for a trout to catch an artificial fly than a real one. You make yours sit stiller, and so tempt more. Halfway up this long run there is a clutch of large rocks in the centre of the river and to the left. Near one of them lies a red stone, just under water save when the river is very low. Above it is a devilish place to lodge a fly, but I have never yet known there not to be a fish here when I pass.

Beyond it lie three rock-based pools, deep, rapid and always, until the summer, loud with the sound of water, for they flow into one another over two-foot lips of rock. Here I rarely get fish in the centre of the stream; it flows too strongly early in the year. The trout lie mostly in at the sides and under rocks out from the shelter of which they dart as a floating fly wanders and pirouettes past. I use every stratagem to delay the passage of the fly over the water in places like this; sitting my line on the tops of projecting rocks, casting it so that the fly floats up a small backwater, then into the current at the top of it, and so down again. All these things one learns to do on small waters. The three pools of which I speak are, incidentally, pretty closely treed and consequently most of the casting must be done with a short line, particularly in high wind.

You will sometimes see a salmon move here, but generally only when the level of the water is rising to a flood. Their true refuge and staging point in low water is the next pool above. Here, too, the primroses begin to grow thicker; they make your world a sybaritical, extravagant place to wade in, colouring it as well as scenting the air.

Above these three pools, so bustling, swirling and noisy, lies

THE FINE-SPUN PORTRAIT II

one of the smoothest, most leisurely, most equable, most various, most luminous, deepest and most stylish pools of the river. Creep up to it always, above all during a blink of sun, because in and around it everything is over-clear. Near the surface move the small trout, glinting and splashing as they rise; up from the depths sometimes a big one darts, pauses for a second on the surface, then vanishes into the dark.

Its first twenty yards are over undulating, smooth yellow rocks, volcanic, old as time, polished smooth by the water. Then on the left-hand side, in the water, stand half a dozen huge smooth uncovered boulders, three of them flat-topped, which one uses to step into the centre of the river, and upstream. The left bank is a rocky cliff, thirty feet high, covered with sallies and a few ash trees; at the bottom of the cliff the run to the top of the pool begins. It is about twenty-five yards long, swift and deep; a pretty place.

There is some shelter under the cliff, and one can back comfortably into it out of the wind and the rain, and out of sight of anyone or anything coming up or down the river. It is one of my favoured lunching grounds because a spring of clear sweet water flows out of the heart of the rock. If you lie still, too, sometimes a kingfisher passes close; once three years ago one pitched suddenly on a bough four feet from me, and for ten seconds glittered like an emerald and preened, then becoming conscious of me, vanished.

To fish this pool, one must wade very quietly because here particularly in the clear, clear water scared trout darting upstream scare their fellows. I walk delicately, making hardly a ripple, and first drop my fly to float along the very edge of each of the great stones; then a little farther out. In to the left, under the cliff, is a small backwater bay which I fish blind – dropping my fly over the top of the tallest protruding rock; it is overhung with trees, and to fish it one risks a fly each time. It is curious to listen for the splash, then strike; but it rarely produces a fish.

Next one mounts the stepping stones, one by one, fanning out casts from each, all over the stream, watching all the time for a rising, moving fish. To the right of the pool is a broad backwater along the side of the current, ending in a bank of gravel. On the edge of it, near the current, facing towards you there is often a fine trout, but you rarely get him because he sees you first, even on the days when the light is bad.

But the real place from which to fish this fine salmon resting pool, though not for salmon, is the last flat rock of the midstream clutch, the one farthest upstream. I walk to the very edge of it – inevitably, I have walked off the edge of it once in a moment of abstraction, so I know the pool to be about eight feet deep at that point – and yard by yard, fan out my casts upstream as far as my rod, the weight of my line, and the wind will let me. It is one of the few places on the lower reach where one can do this with impunity with no trees behind and no obstacles in front; but first choose your day! In eight years I have only fished it once in really favourable, comfortable conditions.

It is too easy, in fact, for my enthusiasm for a loved one to cause a picture of a river to arise in the mind which is remote from reality. You may have the impression, as I recall my clear picture of the Truim, of a man wandering wild in ideal circumstances, easily extracting trout the size of prize turbot from fascinating, pretty waters. This is not true. Always one must recall that the average cadence is nine hours for at the most half a dozen fish, and fingers stiff with cold most of the time. But on very many days, with infinite trouble, the answer is one or none, even for a hard-bitten, durable, crazed fisher, the entire day. There is no visible movement, which is hard; even when one knows that in cold-water rivers in high country early in the season trout take dry fly in conditions in which no fisherman on a southern chalk stream would bother even to go out of doors. Most of the fish that are got are got by intelligent fishing of the water, without ever seeing a rise.

This salmon pool gives way to a steeply flowing run, stony and slippery, to be waded straight up the centre, in and out of quite deep holes, watching, watching all the time for movement around any protruding or barely-covered stone. At the top the river turns half left and is overhung with trees; but it is also one of the few spots where, even on a furiously windy day, fishing is easier; a small protected corner, the fly hatch is more visible because less completely scattered by the wind, so the trout here have the habit of rising more freely.

An incident at this corner a few years ago had nothing to do with trout. I saved a lamb from drowning. It had slipped on a stone as it crossed the stream with its mother, became waterlogged and when I arrived was lying hopelessly on its side, just keeping its nose above the surface. I picked it up and wrung it out like a bath sponge. Mother, meanwhile, was baa-ing hysterically as though she were witnessing murder, and rushing up and down the bank like a lunatic. When I set the lamb down near her and left it, she stood for a moment silent, then quite suddenly made what I took to be a rather emotional congratulatory speech that lasted for about two minutes. I stood in the middle of the river, bowing and occasionally bleating in a genteel, self-deprecatory manner, until quite suddenly she realized she might be making a fool of me, called the whole thing off, and they trotted away.

A series of pleasant, small, quite deep rock pools lie above this corner. The first and the last of the series are the best, though I prefer the first. You fish it from the centre of the stream at the outflow. A big stone, weighing several tons, lies across the pool, overhanging the water at a point directly opposite to you as you stand watching for rises, and a deep hole has been dug by the water between the rock and the outflow. Keeping the fly very low, I fish every inch of this pool, the last cast going right under the rock, with the line collapsed over the rest of the now disturbed water, in order to let the fly stand in the rock's shadow among the backwater flotsam, lifelike and, if you are a fish or an informed fisher, highly inviting.

Trees circumvent casting on these picture pools and hold you close, and real fishing is scarcely practical on more than one day in four. The wind sees to that. The top pool is all confused water with a few protruding stones and spurs of rock. I stand on a half submerged ledge on the shore, that I chose the first time I ever walked that way, and drop the fly down again and again into the current where it sits only for a second before it vanishes in the swirls. But that has often been long enough for a trout to see it.

The true primrose path of Truim lies on the next stretch of the river. Fishing it, I feel cosseted and decorated and deeply obliged to nature for her surpassing arrangements. It begins with a stickle, sixty yards long, rock-strewn; again, a place where an observant person takes a line straight up the centre and follows it, casting right and left, watching for promising rocks and stones near which to let fall a fly. There is one such fine stone in the centre of the river and slightly to the left, about forty yards up. But in the main, someone fishing this long stickle – or any long stickle – needs to watch one thing only apart from the details of movement of the fish, the fly on the water, and the placing of the stones round which the water flows, and that is the course of the main current of the river. Always, where it is, where there is a more emphatic, marked flow of water, the channel that contains it is deeper, and the stones that lie near it will be more promising spots near which good fish will take up position.

The stickle ends in a long double run, quite deep, hedged in on either side by trees, where the taking trout all lie in the fast water. One stands knee deep, waiting for the wind to drop for minutes at a time, sometimes cursing a little. It is probably worth the wait, though to set a fly on this run without drag is a difficult thing, and the trout are quick to notice false movements.

Alongside the top of this run grows a small, proud dwarf oak with umbrella-spread branches so tidy that it is almost like a tame, trained, pollarded resort tree underneath which lies another of my remembered white sheep-skeletons, the meat off which I have watched the years devour and the wool vanish strand by strand. In its carrion year the whole river around it stank with corruption, and I twice saw a guilty cringing collie dog there, that had escaped its far-off whistling master to feed on the carcass. I never sensed in beast or human such acute consciousness of guilt. When it saw me, it belly-crawled to the carcass and gulped the foul meat standing, looking nervously at me over its shoulder from time to time, then slunk away.

I walk up the right bank of the river now for fifty yards, beyond this skeleton, murdering primroses at every step, then slip into the water again through the screen of trees to cross over and fish an excellent but difficult pool, dominated by a large mossy boulder, weighing about one and a half tons, in the middle of the stream. It is a place where, when the Olives are hatching, they fall thickly. The main current flows just to the left of the boulder where the water is deepest, but it is pretty deep even as far as three yards to the left of it. The thing to do here is to fish the tail of the pool first, right across the stream, then the main run to the left, then the secondary run to the right. Each of these can produce a fine trout, but rarely both on the same day. Catch one fish and the others telepathically or physically are disturbed. The final series of casts in this pool should all be round the boulder itself, one to the top end, to float the whole length of it, two inches from it, then a second; then one in front of the boulder searching, searching all the time. It is a pool that never shows a rise except when the Olive is up, but one should fish it carefully, even when no trout are showing. They are there.

After this pool there is some broken water, then another forty-yard stickle which I generally fish from the middle of the river like the one before it. For me, this stickle is famous for two things. First, five years ago, in the field on the left bank, I was bitten by a small white horse which crept up behind me quietly, meanly and with malice and nipped me hard on the left cheek of the bottom. I was, I suppose, contemplating some small absorbing incident in the water, a squadron of tiny mallard chicks, a particularly obsequious dipper, or a water rat grooming himself, Brummel-like, on a mossy stone, and did not notice him. It was a mean trick and I explained this to him in short, horrible words. We never met again.

The second was a fish. I caught him six years ago, one of the really large ones I have taken out of the Truim. About halfway up the stickle there is a fair-sized stone with a cleft in it which has filled with thin earth, from which grows a single hazel switch. I cut it each year the first time I pass it. Two feet to the right and a little downstream of it is a smaller stone, almost covered by the water which just slops over the top of it when the river is at its normal height.

It was a very windy day, but the sun kept blinking out. I did not know the river very well at that time, and I stood in the water watching the second stone just above which a fish kept rising. It did not look a deep-water place. The fish lay opposite to the top of the larger stone, and as an Olive came down, he floated with the current and sucked it in discreetly just above the second stone. I thought it might be a good half-pounder, nothing more; so I battled with the wind for a couple of minutes before getting my fly to the right spot. The fish did exactly what he had done before, following the fly down and taking it in the last split second.

His first jump was right over the big stone; then he ran across the river on the surface of the water, like a rainbow, jumped again, made off downstream, then stopped abruptly near a rock. I thought he was off, so reeled in tight and edged backwards down the centre of the current until I was below the spot, then walked over cautiously to where he had last been seen. He lay dourly, obstinately suspended in the current in front of the rock, the sun lighting up his bright, spotted flank. He saw me and exploded upstream for twenty yards, then suddenly stopped. It was a mistake and a bad one. I let the current carry him easily down towards me, on a tight line, while I unhitched my net. Seconds later, he backed into it. I ran ashore and weighed him in at three pounds seven ounces!

The rest of a day is tame after catching such a trout; he was a cock fish, thick in girth, short and stumpy. I have never had one like him on the Truim since.

Nevertheless, the river continues. Fifty yards farther on, stranded in the centre of the stream, lies an island, like a long, thin green tongue covered with grass and rushes. At the top of it, dividing into two parts a pool three yards wide, lies a big rock backed by a partly hidden tree trunk, which was flood-jammed behind it many years ago. The rock and the tree between them have caught a varied collection of strange objects over the years – parts of a coil of barbed wire, sacks, bits of wooden fencing, and every year drowned ducks, and rabbits and an occasional lamb.

Fish rise all round the rock and the approaches to it. The game for the fisher is twofold; to hook them, then to keep them out of that treasure chest of snags round the rock. It isn't easy. One has to be rough, resourceful and handy, instantly tightening hard when a good fish takes. One in three you manage to turn before they break your cast.

This part of the river, in addition to everything else, is fished to music. The first time you approach it, absorbed in what you are doing, watching the water at the tip of the green island, you hear an extraordinary thrumming and drumming. It vibrates in your ears, and penetrates your mind, distracting and disturbing, but with charm. As you move forward to a pool that lies under an oak tree, deep, rocky and difficult of access, the sound grows louder. As you climb the bank and fish the next pool, for here begins a small stepped waterfall, musical in itself, greatly frequented by kingfishers, the thrumming gets louder. Then suddenly, up above you, you see, many-stranded and majestic, the high-tension wires and you realize that the sound that accompanies all that you do, loudly or softly according to the state of the wind, throughout that whole square mile, comes from this great harp we have stretched across the moor. In high wind its sound is an immensely mournful, wild, piercing public song. On quiet days it keens penetratingly and almost privately to itself. On all days it is curious music to which to unhitch flies from the trees in which all along this bank I tangle so easily. I often lie down here among the heather, in a dip which is nearly always out of the wind, and rest for a time and sup whisky, festive under my suspended harp, then catnap for a quarter of an hour. It's as good a sound to wake to as to sleep to.

For long now, if you have fished these three and a half miles of water in a day, you will have been tired. Your food will probably be down to some least-loved relic, perhaps a dry cracker and cheese; your throat will be a little parched, though at least five

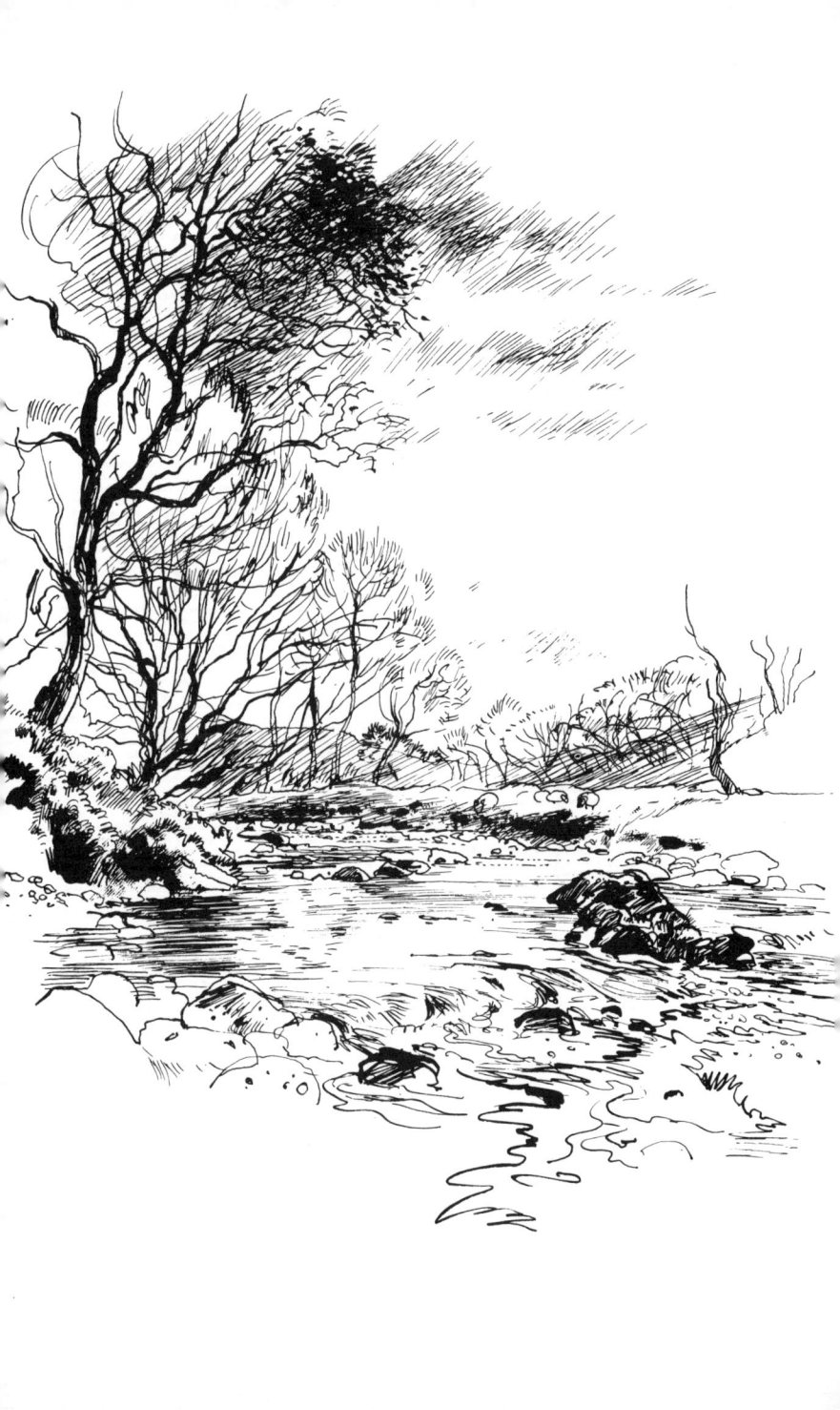

days out of ten you will be wet to the skin. You need a little summoning of strength for your last mile and a half, and some pretty water, including the Falls of Truim.

Precisely under my harp, the river turns sharp left. In the angled, smooth, swift corner pool, bisected by a jagged five-yard spur of rock, tufted here and there with grass, up the centre of the river bed, there are always good fish, though you catch them, I find, only about one season in three. To the left of the spur is an outflow pool, not deep, in which the fish lie mostly at the end of the rock. But the main current flows to the right of it, not the left. In this current the trout lie either in the centre of the pool, or up the right-hand side, which is rocky. I fish them first from the rock spur, wading alongside it. At the end of it you are out of reach of tree-snags and when the wind lets you, you can spin out long casts all over the pool with ease. It is curious that the stomachs of the trout caught in this pool contain a majority of dark flies, though the ones one always sees them take are Olives. This is in fact a Black Nymph pool when the Olive fails; yet the pleasure of seeing the pale, elegant, yellow-green Olive float down past a rising trout always makes me neglect to put on a Black Gnat first. Why be sensible, after all?

Leave this corner, walking through fifty yards of gay, green hazel copse, carpeted with moss, and in front of you lies another long salmon resting pool, a beauty. You keep to its left bank, being careful of the trees on your own side of the river as you fish. The direction of the pool – almost due north and south – and the open field upstream of it makes it a hard one to fish because of the prevailing wind. It can only be done accurately one day in ten at best, but it is worth it. The first twenty yards are seemingly smooth water, but if you watch a twig jazz down it, you know that the speed of the current deceives you, so you should fish the whole of it. Your bank is rocky and you keep to the ledge as you wade, reminding yourself, subconsciously, if a non-swimmer, that one eager step to the right will drop you neatly in the water, up to your neck; the wading must be stealthy, waveless. About halfway down the pool which is some thirty yards long, to the left, a small promontory of rock breaks the surface. Beyond it is a backwater a yard and a half across above a jagged rock shelf. The main current of the pool flows past this backwater and this promontory, proceeding right from the head of the pool which at the top flows fast. The pool is quite broad at the inflow, and there is a current and a backwater on the far bank as well as the near.

I fish this pool yard by yard, for the second biggest fish I ever took in the Truim came from it. There is also a tree-stump on the right bank – it is rotting away now – perched upon which I came, one day four or five years ago, on a disconsolate buzzard. He sat there, evidently broken with age or not entirely right in the head, and watched me apathetically as I fished, never once moving, save for his eyes. He was still there when I left the pool to fish the fast series of runs that lead to the long high-banked approach to the Falls of Truim. In retrospect, another explanation of the buzzard's conduct has occurred to me. He may have been a poacher, trying to sit there innocently while a sporting gentleman strolled by, unaware that his gaff and snare lay concealed behind him in some bushes.

Walking up the field beyond this spot, talking to the sheep which abound there, I keep a look-out for two red deer, I think somebody's house pets, which occasionally appear among the conifers on the far bank and spy on me, possibly to make private observations about my dishevelled appearance or my fishing. A deer in high season is a neat, trim creature with appealing, vacuous, liquid country eyes; so I suppose it has a bourgeois right to criticize untidiness.

I fish the sixty-yard-long runs and stickles here a thought perfunctorily. I am probably wrong, but I am generally tired at this point. The wind has blown me for six hours, the water has dragged at my feet for six hours. I am no longer fresh, and tend to hurry a little to favourite places. It would be different, I suppose, if I started my fishing at this spot; were I, say, as one day I must be, too old for long days and hard work.

Were this so I would wade these long runs quietly and carefully up the current, searching for trout, as always among the humped stones. But normally I do not. I go quite quickly to the corner pool where an enormous round boulder, embedded up to its mossy equator in gravel and water, lies where it rolled, probably centuries ago, to the foot of the high, sloped, treed river bank.

The water here flows fast, so you must stand right at the end of the outflow, and fish short on both sides of the rock. It is a turbulent stream and your line will inevitably sink waterlogged as you run your fly down the edge of the rock, waiting for that small, deliberate, hardly seen, underwater big-fish movement.

Once, four years ago, before this whole stretch was wantonly cyanided by a band of rogues for a single salmon, the trout came thick here, and one evening beside this stone I hooked and broke in a fine fish. I put on a new fly and in three more casts hooked and landed this same fish and got back my first fly. That I hurry to this pool, this rock, is only because I remember that evening and the shock of surprise that a trout of a pound and a half should be such a fool. The fishing there has not yet nor probably will it again for many years recover, since all animals have a long secret memory for disaster.

Beyond this, that I call the stone pool, the river turns sharply to the left, and has a high cliff bank, rocky and with a few heroic trees clinging to it. After twenty-five yards of shallow run a long, smooth pool opens up, dark, oily and secret, where the river emerges from the long cut leading to the Falls of Truim. You cross it early, otherwise the water becomes too deep for wading. You must cast backhanded as you come to the first pool. The railway runs close by, and as I wade and fish here, concealed, and a train roars past, there is a heightening of pleasure in the fishing to remember that other less happy people are returning to Perth or to London. I always feel part of the country and utterly separate from cities until the very moment when the Night Scot pulls me into Euston Station.

At the top of this dark pool, the river turns right, almost at a right angle. I must fish here from the right bank, still backhanded, because here again the trees hem you in, until I reach a point opposite to where a rocky ledge protrudes. Then I move nearer to the centre of the river, and with care return to normal casting, though I must still measure my line to the trees. The best trout at this point move two yards upstream from this ledge and along the sally hedge beyond it, but they have always been hard to catch.

After you have finished here, you have the two- or three-hundred-yard run or series of runs, between high treed banks, leading to the first pool of the Falls of Truim. It is a dark, echoing place and above the noise of the river and the song of the birds you can feel the immanent hill silence. The banks are thickly treed and the wading chancy; you have to go from side to side, watching your step and the trees carefully, fishing where you can. Then the river opens up and turns leftward in a long, dark pool, narrow, clear and swift, in which the trout are seen easily but very difficult to move. Beyond it, where the river again bends sharply to the right, is the first broad, black, deep pool of the Falls. In it you can wade out only a few yards, for it is deep and rock-encompassed. Lie on top of one of the rocks and look down on it on a sunny day and you will sometimes spot a salmon, waiting pretty calmly there to be poached, whosoever can manage it. But in it the trout rise charily.

The falls themselves, now visible from the right bank of the pool, are a lovely series of runs and pools and waterfalls, deep, musical and clear, but also violent and secretly waiting for the man in metal-studded waders whose foot may slip on a rock and drop him into eight feet of swirling water. Here, in shadow, the water is black as its hidden purpose; in the open it is cheerful, gay and diamond clear.

The river here drops a hundred feet in about 250 yards, among a tumble of rocks and stone buttresses projecting from the earth. The banks are high. On the right bank, all the way up, is a conifer wood, the ground under the trees softly padded with fallen spines on which even heavy men must walk lightly. To the left, at the top, lies the road and the railway line, both unseen but heard.

It is hard to fish dry fly in the falls. The rocks near the water slope too deceitfully. It is very easy to scramble down to the water's edge or near it, to find that there is no spot there upon which your feet can gain purchase while you cast. To climb back, equipment dangling, I have often had to take off my waders. Getting down to the water is one thing; climbing back is another. But it is no less worth trying for being difficult; halfway up the falls there is a long turbulent pool, the water rolling and boiling at the head, brilliant and transparent at the outflow, from which every trout you manage to filch will be half as fat again for its length as a trout in any other part of the river; but remember, I average only one a year there.

From this pool you can see the Falls Bridge, very elegant and graceful, enhanced by its setting, like a pretty woman. I fish the approach to the bridge – a short smooth stone-flanked pool – from the left bank, then scramble through the landward arch of the bridge and out to the final stretch of river leading to Crubenmore.

Incidentally, above the bridge lies a swift, narrow run in which I have only once caught a fish, and beyond it two singularly gracious small rock pools, with heather and broom on their banks, so that they are always festively coloured and full of magical reflections. It is in these two pools particularly where the hatch of the Olive is often ignored when it takes place. I stand beside the bridge admiring them and resting for a moment, to change to a black nymph. At least they rise to this, though the number of trout I have taken here over the years is small.

The home stretch is nearly all fast-flowing water, stickles and runs and two or three good pools, passing through green sheep-fields, hedged off from the river by wire. A hundred yards above the bridge lies the Falls poachers' long-established fireplace, black stones with logs half-burned, crooked sticks for holding pots and gear, and the bitter scent of burnt wood.

Here a long, smooth run, upon which there is a big Olive hatch most seasons, leads to a broad pool, best fished, owing to its underwater conformation and the flow of the stream, from the centre of the river, gradually moving over to the left bank. The wind on nine days out of ten makes this pool a trial to fish; it is completely naked and unprotected, not a tree between it and the prevailing wind.

What follows, above it, has long been a lesson to me. It is precisely one of those places past which one walks quickly and carelessly, looking down from the low bank on to the broken water. One says 'It is not worth fishing'. One is lazy and does not wish to skid down the bank. The excuses are all there. In fact, waded upstream, this stretch is completely open, easy to fish, and there are lies for good trout everywhere among the stones and shallow, stepped pools. Halfway along it there is a line of sallies on the right bank of the river, flanking a swift pool; it looks a pretty moderate spot, but in fact it is one of the surest bets for a pound fish in the Truim.

You have turned now, in green country, towards Crubenmore Bridge, lying 150 yards upstream from the last bend on the lower stretch of the water. There is one more spot to fish before the bridge – a small run under a tree, twenty yards from it – and I generally splash up the stream to it pretty thankfully, fished out, like an overfished river.

I treasure a picture in my mind of the setting of this bridge, shaped like the skeleton head of a horned ram, the central buttress being the skull and the two arches the curve of the horns, the old disused bridge just beyond it, the clump of white cottages to the right of it and the cheerful traffic on the road, as a place where I have shown good catches to many people from Dalwhinnie who have come to fetch me home. They are familiar figures, leaning over the bridge looking out for me on fair days, crouched in the car on foul, and on late days even whistling me with a sheep whistle.

Mr Matheson, stout and very joyful when I have done well, and in a modest seemly fashion, pleased that a place he loves should have been prodigal to a friend; Hugh, his eldest son, now owner of the Loch Ericht Hotel, tall and red-haired, with his quizzical slanted smile; Chrissie his wife, small and precisely featured, whose wedding to him I attended in London at St Columba's; Katy, his married daughter, fair, witty, shy, and with great laughter in her, accompanied in the car by Tipsy, a small, nervous, elegant golden spaniel; dark Ian, his younger son, and Ian's wife Bunty who now keep their own hotel by Loch Duich on the road to Skye. They are dear to me as people who have fetched me, evenings, from Crubenmore Bridge, soaking wet, and, driving home, listened to me talk rubbish or sense – one never knows truly which it is – about the undoubted splendours of the day.

ERICHT DIVERSION

This tale of Loch Ericht is written partly to break the journey from the Spey to Dalwhinnie, partly to avoid monotony in a narrative which deals all the time with the same range of things; though nobody surely would read a book on trout fishing unless they were either daft about it or wanted to learn about it, or were making a study of this particular abnormality for medical purposes and wanted to be better documented about its symptoms.

Apart from these reasons, what I call the day of the great fish is vivid in my mind and worth recording. It should be told once and for all, as it has been told and considered by Davy Craib who works on the railway and ghillies on the loch on free days, by myself, by Donald Grant; and by almost anyone from Dalwhinnie who fishes or will listen. It is a tale that has been chewed like a bone. I have used the substance of it in a short story. It has, in fact, by several paths, entered history.

Every year I drag myself away from the Truim to pass a day on Ericht. The wind and the rough water, the colours, the large magnificence of its containing hills, the small bays, the rocks, the green promontories, the great round holes in the bank of the loch hollowed out by the waves, the varied forests, the feeding streams, the deer, the bird-life, the lone lodges and bothies, live easily in my mind, associated with long days, generally cold and wet, fishing that dour, admired water with old friends. One renews this pictured life by taking, from time to time, a day in a boat on the loch. Written down, it may seem too fresh and clear, too burnished; too set up and dusted – to the point of sheer unreality – for those to whom a lake is just a lake, a collection of standing water.

The day of the great fish was four years ago, the last day of my season at Dalwhinnie, a Sunday. Davy Craib took me out since Donald Grant, who was to ghillie for me that day, was ill. I got up in the early morning and caught at Loch Grant fingerling trout for dead-baiting on the troll. The morning was blustery with early flurries of rain, and the wind almost certain to rise with the sun, if the sun rose. After breakfast Mr Matheson drove us over to the green boathouse on the left bank of the loch in the station wagon, with our food, rods, extra clothing and the outboard motor piled in around us.

Davy has the same, excellent non-committal quality about him that Donald has, and the same kind of reserve. In appearance he is sandy-haired with a round freckled face. He smokes a pipe between regular teeth, wears a big watch chain, and is a gentle, solid, easy person to be with for a long day, for he absorbs events, great and small, with wordless pleasure. On the way to the loch we start level, both of us being certain, whatever happens, of a good day.

We baled out the night's rain from the white boat, loaded our gear, set up the engine at the stern, and pushed off from the shore, Mr Matheson watching us and waving from the bank, as he always does. There is something about the Loch Ericht Hotel outboards which gives him less than entire confidence in them, so he waits to see what happens. They are elderly with psychological lesions and wills of their own, which he acknowledges but does not try to cure, nor deeply deplores. So they command the day.

On this particular day, nothing at all could be done with our engine. Davy, with his starting lanyard, pulled and sweated; the boat drifted with the wind even with me rowing hard to keep it reasonably near to the boathouse and the shore. After an hour, we gave up and came in to discuss with Mr Matheson whether to try another engine. But by now it was eleven thirty; it would take an hour to fetch it; and how long to start it? Nobody knew.

So we abandoned the idea of going down to the Corrivachie tunnel because I was taking the train back to London at six that evening. There would never be time to go there and back, and have some fishing. Instead we decided to do what I had done only once before, with Donald, to troll the upper end of the loch.

As we left, the very bottom seemed to fall out of the clouds. I watched Davy's face streaming and steaming as he rowed us away, the rain hissing, the loch white with raised rain-spindrift. A veering, wicked wind gusted and pulled and the clouds rushed overhead like blown smoke from far fire-breathing chimneys. But though we took round striking-stones with us, we forgot the big net that leant against the timber beam of the boathouse. The storm brained us as surely as one brains a rabbit.

We floated out, waving to Mr Matheson through the murk; he was happy and smiling now. At least Davy would not break down. Fifty yards from the shore, at about a quarter to twelve, I baited up the trolls, two shining small trout on swivel tackles, tails kinked and hooked up to give them a wavering movement in the water, and let them out on sixty yards of line. It was rough and windy as well as wet and we hunched our shoulders and pulled our heads down into the necks of our sweaters, like turtles.

Davy took the boat slowly in long undulating reaches, in great S-shaped turns and twists, along the leftward shore, a few hundred yards out. The two rods – old sea-rods of mine – protruded from the boat on either side, the striking-stones holding down their taut lines on one of the seats, the line itself spun out astern, far behind us. I can always imagine the bait turning and fluttering far away in the depths.

After twenty minutes, with a snap of the stone and a piper's skirl, one reel ran. I picked the rod up and felt it as Davy reeled in the other to avoid tangling.

'A small one,' Davy commented.

Five minutes later we netted the fish, a nice two-and-a-quarter-pounder, and as we did so Davy said, smiling:

'Your net's no very large. I don't know what we'll do when we get the big one.'

We wetted our first catch with tots of whisky, put down new baits and rowed on. Turning into the bay beside a long, yellow sandy bluff that can be seen on the left bank of the loch almost from Benalder came our second fish, on the same rod as the first. You could see that it was a bigger one the moment it took; the reel screamed and as I picked up the rod the fish stopped for a second, turned, hesitated, then ran again.

'That's a better one,' said Davy, delighted with us. 'Be easy with him.'

I let the fish run a little then put some pressure on him and he swam slowly towards the boat, diving deep as he came.

'He's all right,' said Davy; 'but no very big. A nice fish, mind you.'

Soon the line was vertical, right beside the boat, springing taut from the water to the head of the short stumpy rod. I worked him slowly towards the surface, and saw Davy from the corner of my eye straighten the net, lay it down beside him and take up the oars again, to keep the boat between my fish and the wind so that I could watch him more easily. The fish rolled, a very fat, broad-backed trout, then seeing Davy and me for the first time, dived in fright, as fish do the first time they see their captors. Five minutes later he was lying quietly on his side, moving only very gently. Davy ran the net over him, tail first, turned it with his wrist, lifted, and the fish was in the boat.

He weighed four and a half pounds and was a fine fish, though he had a curious deformity. Three-quarters of the way down the back, not far above the tail, there was a kink in his body that had stunted his growth. His fore part was that of a six-pounder, the after part that of a three-pounder, though the tail was the tail of a larger fish.

Davy and I wiped our hands on an old towel from my bag and felt a thought pleased with ourselves; an hour's fishing, two fish, six and three-quarter pounds. We had another tot; I watched the rain drip from the end of Davy's nose, and he watched it drip, presumably, from the end of mine. We shivered but were not miserable.

'Never two without three,' said Davy, as he took up his oars again. 'They're on the take; we might do it,' he added.

Twenty minutes later, in the worst flurry of rain yet, came the answer. We were half a mile down the loch from the bluff. I was saying something to Davy about a squall of wind that was coming towards us up the loch when a striking-stone fairly bounced in the air and the reel of the same rod that had caught the other two fish screeched, stopped for a fraction of a second, then ran straight on for two or three seconds more.

'There's a big one,' I said, seizing the rod.

Davy, his oars shipped, nodded as he reeled the other in.

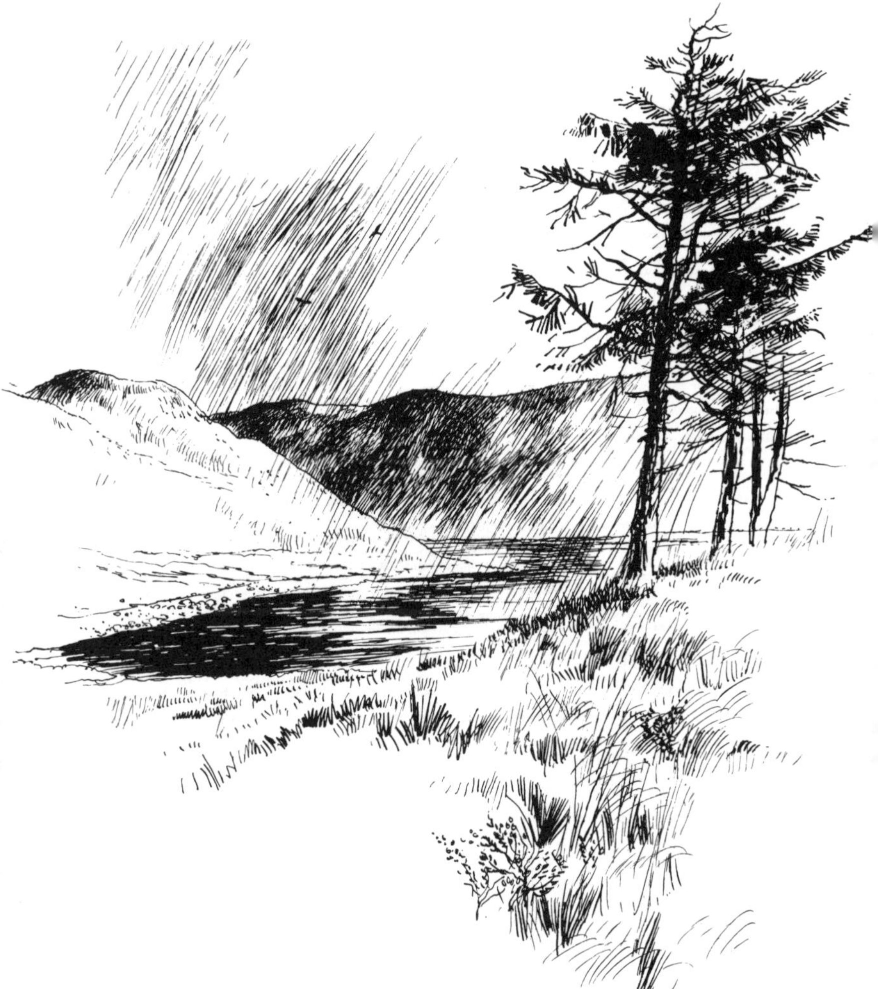

'Aye,' he said, 'and what about the net? And no gaff.'

'We'll play him dead,' I said, cheerfully. So Davy sat down to his oars and we played him. Davy's job was to hold the boat steady in the rising waves.

At first our fish quietly towed us along, in the same direction as the wind. Whenever I had reeled in half a dozen yards of line, he ran again, taking ten. But after twelve minutes, yard by yard, standing up in the boat back to the wind, I began to get back line. The fish never showed himself and kept right away from the boat, then suddenly he dived deep, and Davy had to keep rowing hard, upwind, to stop him from running under us. I looked at Davy over my shoulder; we were both nervous.

'That's a big fish, Mr John,' said Davy.

For another five minutes he swam slowly round the boat, sometimes trying to get under it, sometimes stopping for twenty seconds at a time and shaking his head, trying to throw the bait. Davy kept the wind on my back so that I could watch the fish in relatively calm water near the boat. The rain pelted down, streaming off my hands; the water grew rougher. Then the moment came when Davy said:

'I think we could try and take in some line.'

I nodded, and yard by yard I began to reel in. The fish felt it, but he no longer had the steam in him to take any line back. All I had to do was to reel in two or three yards at a time, give him a rest, then take in another two or three. He cruised more slowly round the boat, no longer stopping to shake his head.

At last we saw him. A great shadow, first, ten or twelve feet down, then as Davy turned to me to say something, suddenly he ran for the surface and took a single glistening, nerve-breaking jump, saw us, dived again, and vanished. I let him have line but he barely took out half a dozen yards. It was clearly the last five minutes. In spite of having held him for so long, I had a feeling in my water that we were going to lose him. Davy was looking round the boat.

'No wire to tail him,' he said, and took up my net, smoothing it and pushing it down inside with his hand as if to make it bigger.

The fish was on the surface now, swimming majestically in small circles, his dorsal fin out in the air, and sometimes even his tail. It was an enormous fin and the body of the fish below showed, as he rolled, close knit, thick and brilliantly shining golden yellow; you could even see his red spots. He was by a long way the biggest Loch Ericht trout I had ever seen except in a glass case; more than ten pounds, I judged, but less than twelve.

'It's a hell of a fish,' said Davy, meaning how were we to net him.

'Let's try the net first,' I said. 'You slip it along the fish with me pulling his head back, then you lift the net.'

'Aye,' said Davy.

The fish came alongside quietly, ponderously rolling, tired, but still very strong. It was perhaps a little too soon to try to net him. Davy very cautiously passed the net over him, but he felt it, splashed violently and panicked, and Davy only just disengaged from him without disaster. He was at least a foot and a half too big for the net.

'Damn!' I said. We were both nervous now. 'Let's let him swim round for another two minutes, then try to tail him.'

Davy took a handkerchief and wrapped it round his right hand, then I brought the fish in again. He lay on his side, well hooked as we could see from the flight in his mouth. Davy put his hand slowly into the water, and with a quick thrust grasped for the tail, but missed. The fish darted off again. We swore.

'Maybe we should tow him to the shore?' Davy suggested.

I turned it down. We had drifted to the middle of the loch and the wind was as strong as anything I had been out in on Ericht. It would be a quarter of an hour's row at least to the shore. We decided to bring the fish to the boat again, for Davy to try to get his fingers into the gills, with the net held under him.

This plan seemed to work perfectly. The spent fish came in and I got him well placed beside the boat. Davy got the net into position, and very slowly I put some strain on the fish's head to open the gills. Davy stretched out his hand and I thought his fingers were actually in the gills, but he only touched him. The fish dived, the trace rapped the frayed wooden side of the boat, sawed for a second and broke. The fish was gone!

We could not believe it. We sat for two minutes looking at one another without a word. Davy was miserable; so was I. The rain poured down.

It was the fine fish we already had, I think, that kept us from jumping over the side.

Mr Matheson received us by the boathouse at four o'clock, delighted with our catch, but desolate when we told him of the one that got away. Donald's view is still that we should have towed him to the shore. Davy's is, I think, the same. Mine is that we did not do badly, but given the same circumstances and the same net, I would have played him for five minutes longer, lifted his head very slowly – we were using a strong trace – then as his tail dropped, the net could have been slipped under him.

Anyway, a great fish is no more and no less than a great fish; and that was our day with this one. It was a pity not to land him, but to see and play him was, in many ways, enough.

11

THE FINE-SPUN PORTRAIT III

I have taken refuge several times under Crubenmore Bridge from snow in June. I have dried my glasses while under it many times. Rarely, once or twice only, I have entered it thankfully for shade. It is, whatever the weather, the starting point for the five miles of the top stretch of the Truim to Dalwhinnie.

At the start of the day I slip down the steep green bank from the road, and, as usual, am out of the world. Mr Matheson, when it is he who has brought me, looks over the parapet at me for a minute, sympathetically, waves a hand to the man he knew who has vanished, and is himself gone. I set up my rod, taking pleasure in its strength and slimness, thread the line through the guides, tie on my cast and stand for a moment to watch the water for flies. If it is nine o'clock in the morning and cold, there won't be any. If it is ten o'clock and a pale sun, there will be one or two. If there has been sun in the early morning, whatever the weather, even snow, there will eventually be a hatch. In May, the best thing to do is to put on an Olive and hope for the best, but keep an eye out for Little Iron Blues, for if they appear, the fish generally feed on them easily for an hour or two.

I take the right arch of the bridge through which the main flow of the river passes. Like the Laggan Bridge, it has a good echo, and if I am in yelling mood, I have a good yell here also. The trout don't mind, or if they do, their social organization is insufficient to put a stop to it.

The sound of the water against one's waders as one walks

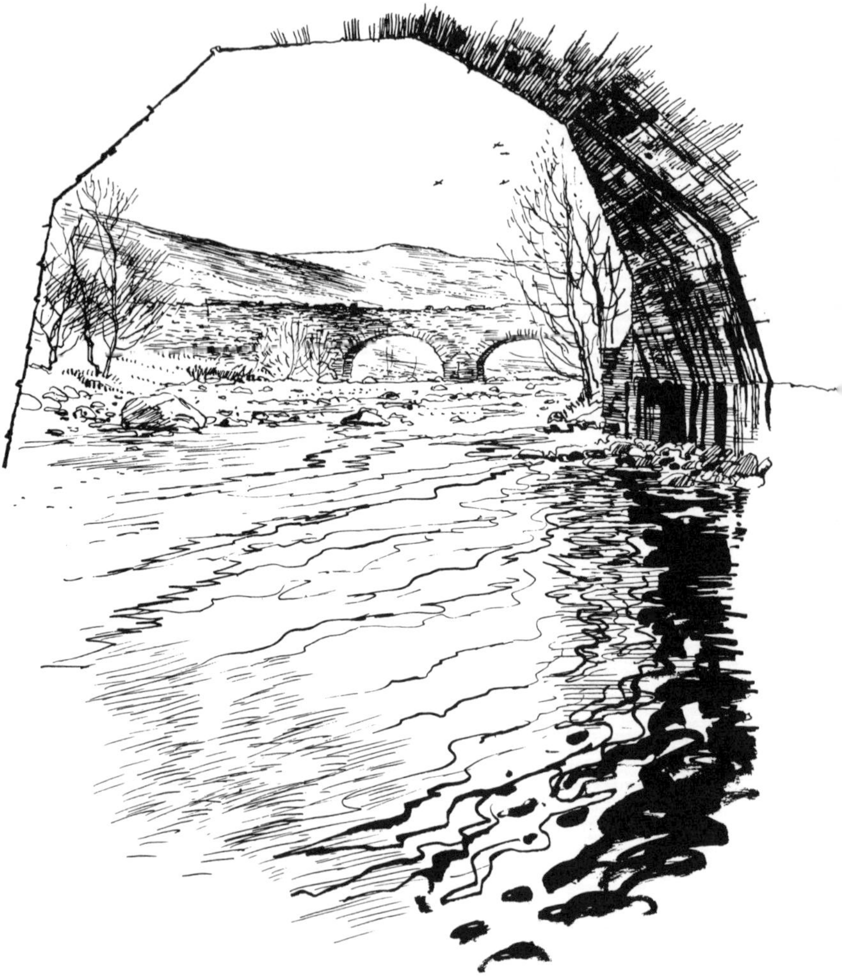

upstream echoes under the vault of the arch. The current is on the left side of the arch, and the pool under the bridge and just beyond it is quite deep. Fish lie all the way up it, but particularly full in the current beside the buttress of the bridge that faces upstream at the top of the pool. If you hook a fish of a pound here, the splash as you tighten on him is tremendously noisy, and you take him for twice his size. If you lose him, of course, he was twice his size.

Emerging from the bridge, I cross towards the left bank after fishing the short run down to the bridge, then walk up the middle of the stream, dropping flies by the stones in front of me as I go. A hundred yards up is the second, old bridge of Crubenmore. Two white cottages lie to the right between the bridges.

The old bridge rarely has a fish under either arch, or perhaps I have little confidence in the bridge as a structure, and so do not fish there sufficiently diligently. It is abandoned, unused and falling down, and I pass under it quickly. Beyond it, though, lies a long, sally-bordered, fast run full of rocks with deep-dug troughs around them. This I fish slowly, quietly and with delicate care.

It is here that you become aware, if you are fishing the upper stretch for the first time, of the devastating quality of the wind. You can stand in the water, rod, cast and fly in hand, often for two whole minutes waiting for a moment to let go in which it will be possible to cast at all. But on a reasonably quiet day it is a beautifully tidy place to fish. As you walk up it, the game is to follow the main current among the rocks round which the best fish lie. At the top of the run on the left a small feeder stream flows in from the hill at right angles; it brings cold snow-water down to the river in May and June from the tops. Just above it is a short swift run with a smallish pool at the head of it, holding a large smooth rock. It is a pool to fish with respect. It runs deep and fast, and I have never known it not to contain a good fish.

To catch that fish, however, is another matter. The only way to prevent drag on your fly is to wade into the full current five yards below the pool, then drop your fly first just beyond the lip of the pool's outflow, then a yard higher, and so on until you reach the rock. The best fish in the pool, for some reason, always floats back with the fly, and if he takes it does so a foot before the fly goes over the edge of the pool into the outflow. The probable reason for this is that there is almost always an unseen drag on the fly and he suspects it of not being real. The great difficulty, and the reason why I rarely land a fish from this pool, is that in the first flurry of tightening on him, the line slackens for a second, and this enables him to run downstream. Since he is nearly always lightly hooked, I often lose him.

All this time you are going up a narrow valley which slowly opens up and broadens, the hills pushing back from you, until you move into what I have taken to be the bed of an ice-age lake. At first the country is green with a few deciduous trees; and all around, holding it in and framing it, are the bold brown and purple hills, white-topped and streaked with old or new snow.

When there is a spring snowfall, you look out of your bedroom window at the hotel and see the sugar-powdered tops and the sheep grazing near the house breathing steam, and curse, though provided the sun shines a little, the rise to natural fly will still take place on the Truim, even in snow. The water is so cold normally that southern dry-fly conditions are no criterion. Two years ago, I took three large trout to a dry fly – an Olive – during a heavy snowstorm in an arctic wind. I was never more surprised in my life; maybe it shocked the fish too.

Beyond this one-rock pool where the fish take as the fly goes over the lip, the river turns a little to the left, towards the railway line and a row of white railway workers' cottages, and forms a long series of pools and stickles, not important-looking when viewed from the bank, but instantly impressive seen from the level of the water. This is a stretch to fish slowly and with care.

First, a single sally bush at the bottom of the series of pools covers an excellent shallow lie. Fish it, then wade on upstream, keeping two yards from the bank. It is very slippery wading because the stones on the bottom are covered with green weed, a regular place for me to fall and fill my waders, soak my lunch and rust my boxes of tackle due to damp, followed by neglect to dry, and I walk with almost elderly caution.

The best place for good fish is about halfway up where three deep, small pools, each with stones showing in them, flow into one another. They are so good that it pays to watch them for a moment or two, and wait before casting. I like to see exactly where the fish are lying because the current is confused in all three pools and since your floating line must lie on the surface of the pool below the one you are fishing, there will only be a small part of a second in which your fly will sit properly, so it must land practically on a trout's head if you are to catch him. On the other hand, a simple refusal of your fly by a rising trout, when there are others of the same kind going past that he is taking, means that your line, unseen by you, is dragging. The moment you drop your fly right on the fish's head and there is no drag, the chances are that he will come at once.

The next stretch of river which turns a corner to the right in a wide arc is largely broken water, with a few good-looking pools, all of which, however, yield practically nothing. I fish there only in desultory fashion as I wade past or scramble along the bank on the escarpment below the railway cottages. The pool worth fishing here is the fine salmon lie about eighty yards long that leads away from the cottages, slightly angled towards the road. The right bank is nearly all rock from one end to the other. The left bank is brown earth, with clumps of bulrushes growing in the water, and about three-quarters of the way along a big stone lies half submerged – one of the few certain places in the smooth part of the pool to rise a trout. It is no use here to fish dry fly to anything save rises, except when you begin to feel the pull of the current against your feet and legs at the start of the run towards the top of the pool.

In late May and early June this part of the river is populated more than any other with extremely diligent mallards. Almost always, coming towards the head of this pool one hears the cheep of mallard chicks and curses, not because they are not pretty and appealing creatures, but because their brave mother will shortly appear and act the broken-winged duck in front of you for ten minutes to distract your attention from them. The Dalwhinnie mallards are, I think, prone to overplay this display of mother love; the place, I suppose, is lonely and there are very few people, relatively, before whom they can show their paces and their awful histrionic gift.

First the chicks appear, a small, tightly packed brown and yellow flotilla, in at the bank. Occasionally one darts out from the line and catches a fly. They are a very business-like little navy, off to somewhere or other in a hurry. Mother, beady-eyed behind a bush or under the overhang of the bank, watches until she thinks that you, the destroyer and marauder, have not observed their escape, then she rushes out zig-zagging all over the surface of the pool, quacking with a note of broken despair in her voice, flapping one wing and letting the other trail, useless, in the water. She then proceeds upstream, supposedly leading you, who are also assumed to want her for the pot or possibly for the duck slave traffic in Buenos Aires, away from her brood.

I often have to wait ten minutes at the head of the pool until the mother has completed her act, though I sometimes chase the chick flotilla downstream, whereupon she may fly round behind me to try to lead me away from them upstream, though this is rare. The current carries the chicks quickly away and her usual plan, quite rightly, is to lead the enemy in the opposite direction, up river.

Even mallard-disturbed, the top of this pool yields good trout. The current runs in the centre of the pool, and is turbulent; the water is deep and the best place to take it is from the left bank, and the backwater on this bank is the best spot in the pool. At most levels of water it enables one to move up the pool sitting the fly on the backwater right alongside the current, thus showing it to fish feeding in the current as well as to those in the backwater itself.

After this pool comes a long stickle which continues, turning slightly to the left towards the railway line, for fifty or sixty yards. Here, I generally cross to the right bank because of a small pool near a sally bush where I once caught a good fish years ago, and have thus an old illusion that I shall do so again. It is really only a small deep hole, dug by the flowing water near a mossy stone. I fish it nevertheless with blank obstinacy every time I pass by, and take pleasure from what I imagine to be its refusal to yield.

Fifty yards farther on, the river is again right beside the railway line. There is a siding with a signal box, and I often fish

FISHING A HIGHLAND STREAM

near it, watched by the people in the trains and by their engine drivers. We even exchange dumb-show civilities. The railway pool is a pretty one and often contains a salmon. It is rocky, and divided into two parts. In the lower half the current runs to the right, with a corresponding backwater to the left; then comes a large rock, and another smaller, more compact pool above it, where the flow of the current, though dominantly to the left, is more diffuse.

The way to fish it – the way I do it, that is; there are many ways – is to take the right bank first. The pool is deep and a yard and a half out you are near the top of your waders. Fish the stream up the current and in the left-hand backwater up to the stone, then go back and cross the pool near the outflow, and fish up the left bank and in the small pool beyond the rock.

As I turn away from this pool, the signalman in the box, if he is visible, often waves to me and I wave back. This piece of country is one where the pleasure of loneliness becomes more acute when people exchange these distant courtesies. There is a special warmth in being perceived.

The river now turns to the right, straight towards the road, and I cross a small feeder burn to reach one of the best pools in the whole top stretch. It is approached by a long stickle, very shallow and chattery. I keep to the bank, and do not wade up it save at the top of the stickle near the outflow of the pool, which is almost round with a broad backwater and a bed of weed to the left, and the main current to the right. At the top of the pool on the right bank is a large black rock with an underwater ledge to it; a yard downstream a small bay forms another backwater. When the prevailing wind blows, which is most of the time, the whole of this small bay is covered with a carpet of foam. I cast my fly heavily into it, so that I can see the mark where it lands. Drag, here, does not matter; it is being seen by the fish beneath the foam that counts, and many gather here to feed.

But it is the main stream and the left-hand backwater that contain the best fish. They must be watched for and spotted carefully, because the pool contains a great many small trout. It is perfectly possible to walk up this pool and get a fingerling trout every two casts. Consequently the thing to do is to move very slowly, watching for a good fish, and put the fly very near to him indeed, if you can. Several years ago, during the hour before the flood water of a thunderstorm near Drumochtar came down the river, I had a three-pounder at the head of this pool. I got a cheer from the signalman a quarter of a mile away as I landed him, and we exchanged congratulatory hand signals across the moor.

It is a curious thing about small rivers like the Truim that there is often some special piece of knowledge which will bring you fish if you use it carefully. It is frequently the same one, namely that the number of fish that lie in at the bank or right under the bank by far exceeds those that lie out in the stream. When that season of the year is reached in which the trout are more generally out in the current, the water is often too low for this to matter.

Most of the fish I catch on the whole of the upper stretch of the Truim from the round pool to Dalwhinnie are taken close to the bank, but because of the bitter wind and the treelessness of the countryside, the number of rises seen is very small. The whole journey upstream for five miles is thus a battle of wits, a guessing game, based on the memory of successes in past years, and finding an answer to the question how to push out your fly, even remotely in the direction you want, into the wind.

Two things, however, I remember as having brought me fish on the worst days. The first is that the Truim does not flow on a straight and regular course. On the contrary, it snakes and serpentines about over the moor, twisting and doubling back on itself. Consequently, if you keep in mind the course of the river, you will know that on windy days for at least part of your long trek you will have the wind behind you. When the wind is very high, therefore, I take with me two reels, one for fishing wet fly – a single fly, usually an Olive – downstream, which I do standing far back from the water, the implacable wind behind me, the other for greasing and fishing dry upstream on the short stretches where the wind helps it.

Nevertheless one learns a lot by persisting in fishing against the wind, upstream in rough weather. After a few years, by controlling the line in one's hand and shooting it in the last split second of the cast, one finds one gets to places which would have been impossible not long before. I rarely fish downstream now, preferring generally to fight it out with the weather, the wind in my face.

Above the round pool begins a series of long runs and pools, mostly over stones and rock, between heather banks, or banks of short-cropped grass bordered with rushes; typical runs in which, at first, one expected to find a trout in mid-stream in May. For me, all this is over. I concentrate on running my fly subtly down the very edge of the banks. You see no rises, or hardly any, and hooking a trout is a thing of instinct. You spot as your fly passes a tuft of grass, or some rushes, or a stone, the smallest underwater movement; if you then tighten, on the second, as your eye registers the movement, you may hook a fine fish. This series of pools does not take long to fish unless it happens that you see open movement and rises, generally when the wind is not high and the fly hatch sits the water in fair numbers.

Just beyond this point the river turns to the left quite sharply, then doubles back in a wide quadrant to the road. It is an exposed spot with long, shallow stickles and runs in which I have rarely caught a trout. It leads, however, into another series of fine pools below the quarry that lies on the far side of the main road to the north, from which you overlook this stretch of river as you drive past.

The main pools of this series are places to fish carefully in warm weather, but only in the flowing parts. The still water produces very little in any weather. When it is cold, as in the rest of the stream, the only places worth trying are the edges of the runs, right in at the bank. Salmon often lie in the deep parts of these pools for a few days after a flood, but never move to a fly.

Just below the quarry there is a feeder stream that runs fast, almost parallel to the road, in wet weather, but makes a row of stagnant pools in drought – which I have once seen! – and between it and the road there is a small, sparse copse of stunted ash trees. This is a resting place for me, because on the edge of the copse sits a pointed triangular slab of stone, upright as a maiden aunt. Its base is at right angles to the prevailing direction of the wind, and consequently you can unload and sit behind it even on the worst days, warm and out of the weather. You eat and for a little time your eyes cease to drop water; you drink a little and optimism returns to you. Conditions, until you step out from behind the shelter, seem more clement.

When you do leave it the river turns half left in a long, stone-bordered stickle with a good bank on the far side, but the place is so exposed that the wind rarely allows one to fish it well. For me it has never yielded many fish, but here I begin to put up a good many grouse and black game as I walk; they start up with a tremendous noise and clatter, and by their jinking flight and startled cries, entertain and compensate me.

The next good pool lies at the foot of a steep bank down from the road, and is one of the finest in the river. It has twenty-five yards of deep, swirling water at the upper end, and a long gradually deepening smooth approach. It is a place for big trout and an occasional salmon. One fishes it from the left bank, at first from the stones, then from the water, but wades carefully since much of the pool is four or five feet deep. On the right bank, all the way up the pool, there is grass or clumped rushes near which one fishes thoroughly, as close to the bank as one can get. But as the water deepens – the main current is to the right – one starts to fish both the bank and the backwater on the left-hand side. In this part of the pool, over the years, I have had several fish over two and a half pounds. Anyway, in May it is always worth most careful fishing, with an Olive.

The river now leaves the near neighbourhood of the road and takes a sharp left turn into the open country with no vestige of shelter or shadow of a tree for a mile or more. There are two quite shallow stickles, then a short run, in neither of which many fish show. I run my fly quietly under the bank once or twice as I go up, just in case I should have been wrong all these years, then after a patch of broken water comes a pool which, although shallow throughout its thirty-yard length, flows quickly and is full of trout feed. It was here, last year, that I caught three fish all over a pound in half an hour during a heavy snowstorm. You will, however, scarcely see a move here in May unless the Olive is on the water. If it is, the pool is one to cover very slowly, yard by yard, not concentrating as I normally do on the edge of the bank, but fanning out casts all over the pool. The fish may be anywhere, right in at the shallow water to the left, in the centre of the stream where the current flows fastest, or under the far bank. There is no telling.

Anti-climax follows it, in the shape of a forty-yard-long, shallow run in which one sees nothing at all. I splash through it, rather fast, stamping my feet a little, having probably stood still for quite a long time in the cold, until I reach a deep round pool at a right-hand turn of the river, where the main current flows to the left. I take the right bank to fish. From my bank, I see the current flowing strongly to the left, and in front of me a broad backwater. It is here that the fish lie, not in the current, and I cast all along the edge of the stream, letting my fly stand still at different points in the backwater, and not be pulled away. The point of the run, where the backwater joins the current on my bank of the stream, is the lie where once or twice I have risen or taken big trout, so best fish it cautiously.

Next, I cross the river, to thirty or forty yards of water which, when the wind is downstream, you can fish with the wind behind you, for the river doubles back on itself. It is a wonderful relief to be able to cast accurately where you wish, and this small stretch of water can be fine fishing, smooth yet fast flowing. All the way along the far bank the water runs deep close in to the side. The bank is green with a pattern of bays and small inlets that changes every year as the banks cave in or are pulled down by the wet fingers of the winter floods. Again, the number of rises seen here is very small, and eyesight is at a premium. An almost imperceptible shift, almost like a change of colour in the water, takes place; one senses it more than sees it, a fraction of a second before the fly reaches a promising spot; then a flash of yellow, a roll and a boil in the water, a tightening of the wrist and your rod is bent like an archer's bow. It is a lovely thing to feel.

But infallibly the river turns left into the wind again, and the easy ten minutes come to an end. Two sleepy pools follow, deep and smooth but quite fast, with crumbling banks and continually changing bays. They produced fine fishing one year about six years ago, but since then they have become another harbour for diligent mother-mallards with their theatrical broken wings. Possibly the impatience these noble actresses arouse in me makes me too cranky to fish well enough to catch the trout that are doubtless still there. Anyway, what I usually do is to carry out a little mallard-spotting before I fish, and if I see or hear one of the chick flotillas and thus expect the worst, I give them a wide berth, so that mother, if she is a lady, which is occasionally the case, can follow her darlings downstream.

The purpose of this stratagem is to protect the admirable corner pool that follows. It is deep, with a disturbed, rolling backwater to the left, and a spit of fine gravel between it and the main stream of the river over by the far bank. You fish the whole pool very carefully, starting with the backwater; then you wade out on to the gravel spit which lies submerged and drop your flies all the way up the current along the far bank. It is at the top of the pool, where a tangled bramble bush trails in the water near where a wet-weather runnel enters the stream, that you should watch for a big fish. You may find one rising there one year in four.

Two deep, swift little pools, then the river turns left to the railway line and doubles back, and again you cross the river on the windy days to fish for 150 yards in classic style in a classic series of smooth runs, with the wind behind you.

This is one of the spots where the fish, early in the year, lie out in the stream as well as in at the bank, so I cast first right at my feet, very short, then fan out as I go, to a cast of about fifteen yards. Only then will I concentrate on floating my flies, close in, down the far bank. In this part of the river the banks have a big overhang of soft earth, and the farther under them you can get, the more certain you are of rising a trout. It is a place to fish yard by yard, until, at the top of the last swift run, you cross the river again and turn right to the first pool beside the railway line.

The Inverness or the Perth and London trains pass it by; and for the visitor at his carriage window I recall that I am a picturesque highland native, a fisherman at his river, and I feel myself pointed out with the same awestruck zoo forefingers that point to the curious doings on monkey hill, or the burning eyes of tigers. Some wave to me and I wave back with dignity. After all, they are leaving me, and graceful deportment sits well even on an untidy squire.

This is a deep pool, swift but calm, and trout lie all the way up it whether in at the bank or in the stream. It is, however, like all the Dalwhinnie railway pools, completely exposed, and the wind knifes through you and blows the cast, over and over again, straight back in your face. It is the only one of the series to be fished from the left bank. At the top of its run I cross over the broken shallow water on to the right bank again. Not, probably, that it is really easier to fish it from that side; it is a habit, induced by a single incident years ago. I saw a big fish rise in one of the pools and could not reach it without crossing the river; now I approach the place by the same way each time I walk that stretch. It has become a ritual habit.

The thing about all these pools is that many of them are edged with rushes and reeds, and in the Truim rushy pools, in May, have the best trout in them, and they generally lie near the edge of the rushes. I go up the middle of the river, dropping my fly beside the clumps of rushes as I pass. The last railway-side pool, on a warm day, is one of the best in the river. It is only about thirty feet long and very narrow – barely ten feet across in most places, and very deep, with a strong current flowing on the left-hand side. Some submerged stones create swirls in the centre of the outflow end of the pool, and the current is very narrow, making a relatively big backwater on the right-hand side of the pool. The bottom is gravel. I fish it from the right bank, generally with one foot in the water and one on the bank, and I send my fly straight up the centre of the pool, not too near the current, but not letting it sit immobile in the backwater. It nearly always works. The fly twists and turns in small circles in the eddies, and if there is a fish on the move, he will come up to look. I never leave the fly on the water too long, but keep moving slowly and purposefully upstream, my last cast being at the point of the backwater where it meets the current at the head of the pool. That is the perfect spot.

After it, the river turns sharp right, and again for a moment you can fish an excellent stretch of water with the wind nearly at your back. It is smooth-flowing and narrow. The grass trails in the water with serpentine movements; the rushes shake in the wind. You walk very carefully, spotting fish, because this is a place where fine trout lie, but they rarely rise noisily and openly. The smallest indication, an unusual movement of any kind in the water, is the thing to watch for. I think after a time on rivers like the Truim, one acquires a sixth sense about unusual movements; I know I have. Part of this stretch is often only four feet across, so even with the wind at one's back it is hard to control the fly.

Here, last year, I hooked and lost a very large fish that ran me thirty yards upstream in five seconds, into the big pool that lies above this run. In another twenty seconds he was clean lost. He took my Olive with a rise so dimpling that I barely saw him come.

The pools that follow lie close to the road. They are deep salmon holding pools, gravelly, and with reddish rock walls on the right bank. They can only be waded at the edges, and must be walked delicately and without a ripple if you are to catch fish in them. There are plenty to be had, though they are not often seen rising except at the end of May.

It is worth stopping and resting at the first of the pools and taking a sup of whisky. As it warms and relaxes, one watches the movement of the water. There are nearly always moorhens on it, but this does not matter. One looks for the small rings of rising fish, what they take, and what fly is on the water, because at this pool the fish are very wary and selective, often, strangely, taking Black Gnats and dark flies when the prevailing fly on the water is the Olive. But if Olives are on and they are being taken, then the fishing here is perfect. They rise generously and can be very big. Over the years, I have had fish on the three-pound mark from this pool, though not recently.

Heavy casting on this pool and the next is not permissible. Your fly has to sit like thistledown and right on your fish's head to make him rise. The clarity of the water and its slow movement in the best parts of both pools allow for no mistakes.

The second of them is the one below the Cuaich Bridge where I caught my first big Truim trout, of which I have already written.

It runs right beside the road, and if the sun is out, sometimes people stop their cars on the small rise overlooking the pool and watch me fish. I try to give them sport before they move on, never once having left their seats.

12

HOT DAY AT CUAICH

Once upon a time, one year, there was a heat-wave at Dalwhinnie. I had fished on a particular day during that heat-wave, in brilliant sunshine, from Crubenmore to Cuaich Bridge, about which I have just spun you the story. The runs had faded to half-hearted stickles, the best pools lay stagnant; and it was only the first week in June.

There were half a dozen people staying at the hotel besides myself and we were averaging about one fish a day each, mostly got by me with dry fly on the loch, late in the evenings. Reaching the bridge on the footpath to Loch Cuaich, I decided to leave the almost empty river and climb to the loch. On the way I got permission from James Christie, the keeper who has charge of it, to fish, though he looked at me as if I was a bit touched by the sun, bothering to climb there on such a day. But I had no fish in my bag, and to climb to Cuaich was something to do.

In the sun it took me well over an hour. I reached the lochan, sunk between two high hills, and that day blue and shining as a sapphire, at around four o'clock in the afternoon. I was tired and sleepy. A few plovers tumbled in the shimmering air; oyster-catchers seemed to fly more slowly, the sheep and lambs looked parched and sat near the water, panting. Taking the footpath on the left bank of the loch I trudged to the far end where the water from the Loch Seilich pipeline forms, on the days when it flows, a deep, rolling pool connected by a channel a hundred yards long to Cuaich itself. Only a trickle of water was coming through now, so

HOT DAY AT CUAICH

I walked beside the channel to the bay to which, when the water is flowing, it gives movement.

The wind had faded almost to nothing – on most casual visits to Cuaich it is an arctic gale, with torrential rain – and I waded out very slowly and lazily into the loch and began to fish with a dry fly, the same Olive that I had been using on the Truim.

I could see the fish moving about in the small, feeble stream from Seilich, and began to drop my fly accurately on their heads with a light cast and soon had four or five of Cuaich's usual three-to-the-pounders.

Then, just as I had decided to go ashore and sleep in the heather under a rock for a couple of hours until the still of the evening when the sun would be off the water, suddenly a big trout showed and took a fly ten yards from me in the barely flowing current. In seconds I covered him, and at the third cast he came up at me, rolling slowly and deliberately, took my fly and made off with it.

Though he was very lively, he was an easy fish to take because the loch is broad and contains few snags. I played him gently, giving him plenty of line, and five minutes later netted him. He weighed three pounds one ounce, a fine cock fish with a very bold trout-pattern on his fat flanks. It was a surprise of surprises, but instead of continuing to fish I found sleep rocking my eyelids, and put my catch in my landing net in the water to keep it fresh, found a shady rock and slept beside it for about two hours.

When I awoke the loch was a deeper blue, utterly silent and without a flicker of wind, but I could hear a noise of water and noticed an increased swirl near the Seilich channel into Cuaich. The valve had been opened a little to transfer some water from Seilich to Cuaich. I almost ran to the entry pool. It was lively and rolling.

Changing to a big fly, a Baigents Brown Variant, I remember, big and buzzing, I entered the water and began sitting it about on the surface of the pool to try the effect. It was lifelike, I thought; were I a fish I'd certainly try it. The next cast, one did!

HOT DAY AT CUAICH

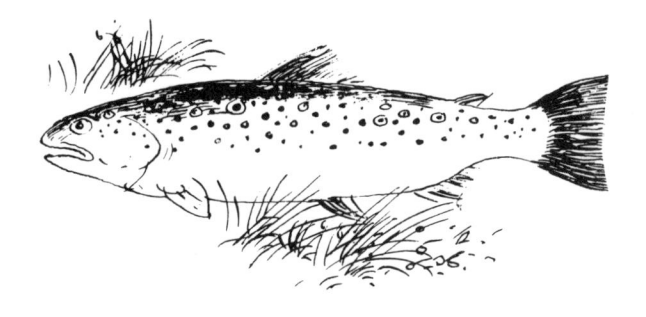

He came up in a flash from right under the inflow where the foam is thickest and whirls most violently, snatched the fly and dived back at the barrier. Though I put instant side-strain on him, nothing could hold him for a fraction of a second, then before he reached the fall, he stopped and dived deep, and remained, I judged, somewhere near the bottom of the pool, motionless. For four or five minutes he sulked there dourly and would not budge. I reeled in tight and walked towards him, having first picked up a pocketful of stones from the bank. First I threw one at the place where the fish was, then another, then a small handful. Nothing happened for a time, then suddenly the fish showed, moving as fast as I ever saw a trout move in my life. He shot past me near the right bank, and dashed downstream, stripping line off my reel at such a pace that I had to run hard to keep in touch with him. I scarcely know how we reached the loch together, but we did. I waded out into the water and forced my fish to swim around hard, by scaring him. He was a big one, and gave in very slowly, but at last, after ten minutes, I managed to reach him with my net and slip it under him. I carried him ashore, crowing to myself, triumphant. He weighed just over five pounds.

Though my bag was heavy, I did not mind the long, hot hour

and a half's tramp home, incidentally in waders, from Cuaich to the Loch Ericht Hotel that night. I was gay and light-hearted and sang to myself, knowing that nature was great, compassionate and merciful, and would forgive the noise, for she had been already exceedingly kind to me on that rare sunny evening at Cuaich.

When I got back, I walked into the bar for a pint of beer, and after the steam as I drank the first swallows had subsided, and the company was eyeing me suspiciously, I said: 'D'you know, I'm the damnedest liar that ever came into this bar! D'you know that?'

Donald Grant, relaxed with cool ale at the end of a hot day, said: 'Come on, man, what the hell have you got?'

I took out the two fish, by a long way the finest brace I ever caught in Cuaich, and laid them out on the bar counter among the pools of beer and the glasses, delighted with myself.

13

THE FINE-SPUN PORTRAIT IV

From Cuaich to Dalwhinnie, though the distance is over two miles, has always seemed to me to be the home stretch of the Truim. You start in the middle of the broad valley in flat, barren land, between the bare hills. The village and the distillery lie in the distance, in the middle of the picture; the road on the right bears its flotsam of cars; the railway line is on the left. At intervals the long trains run by like toys, the echo of their wheels thrown back by the hills. The clouds, the sun, and the sky change the scene from wet and grey to delicate and luminous, all day long. At Dalwhinnie, there are few days devoted to a single kind of weather, with a single quality of light, so there is no possibility, for the seeing eye, of monotony.

One ducks under the concrete Cuaich Bridge with some care. It is very low, and I once miscalculated. Just beyond it there is a swift pool, the right bank of which is shored up with old railway sleepers. I take it from the left bank and fish along the right very carefully, particularly when there is plenty of water, but generally the head of the pool is best. At the top of the run, I cross to the right bank and walk slowly up it, watching for movement among the stones in the broken water which continues for about 150 yards. It is not a place where the trout take readily except close to the bank, so I generally fish this 150 yards only in desultory fashion unless I have time on my hands. This part of the river is fairly shallow, but the banks overhang nicely and a fly running neatly down them, wings erect, dancing among the eddies, turning into the small bays, or riding the rapids past tufts of brilliant green grass, sometimes produces brisk surprises.

The next really promising place, up from Cuaich, is where the river first curves in a wide quadrant to the right, then runs within fifty yards of the road, in a long smooth pool. I wade it from the left bank, and I have taken good fish from it, generally when there is plenty of water, but even so they do not rise at all readily except at the head of the pool near the rocks. All the way along it, however, as usual I search the small bays and inlets on both banks of the river. It is too pretty a place to believe sterile, though I have only taken a fish there once in four years.

Beyond it, within twenty yards of the road and parallel to it, is a deep pool, swirling and disturbed, into which musical springs empty themselves and where the brown turf banks overhang deep, black water. It is about fifteen yards long, and is a rare hatching place for Olives, one of those where they sometimes show really thickly. I fish it from the left side, the only place, one wader in the deep water, one on the bank. The main current is to the right, the backwater to the left, and when the wind lets me I never set my fly in the current, but always in the backwater, so that it rides the very edge of the current, often quite slowly, conjuring out the trout from the current itself. This is a very fine small pool, narrow and fast but badly placed for the prevailing wind; a pretty place to fish all the same.

The river now turns sharp left and a hundred yards separates you from the old iron railway bridge across it. You take the right bank, because being at right angles to the prevailing wind, this is another place where you can fish with the wind behind you most days. The water between the road and the bridge is generally shallow. At the short swift run just after the corner is a bed of trailing grass and rushes. The nearer you can get your fly to them without tangling the better; the big trout hide almost under the rushes here, and I get one, probably at the cost of a fly or two, every other year. It is an easy place to neglect to fish, however, because the river is so meagre and poor-looking, and so shallow. I suspect, even, that most passers-by do not fish it at all.

All along the left bank, up to the bridge, the water is sluggish and I drop casts along this bank, comfortably, with the wind behind me. The pool below the bridge is the one in which there is always at least one big fish, but exceedingly shy, on account of the trains. But I had one there, on a fine sunny day six years ago. He could be seen moving close to the left bank, head-and-tail rolling and taking flies, but the wind was so fierce that it was almost impossible to cover him. Also the place where he was moving was so open that one would scarcely get more than one cast to him; I hit it off, by sheer luck, the first time. I waited until a great gust of wind blew itself out; there was a three- or four-second lull, and I was there. The fish weighed two and a quarter pounds.

Above the bridge, the river runs smoothly in a series of fine pools, but its course turns just after the bridge so that the wind is mostly straight in your face all the way. This is also a great mallard area; at least three clutches are hatched here every year, so often, in addition to the raging wind, you have several excited Bernhardts working against you. The thing to do is to stand still and pretend resolutely not to notice; eventually after awful splashing and scurryings, they swim or fly away to their children, leaving you alone.

This is a part of the river to fish in leisurely fashion or beside which to spend an afternoon. Its half dozen or so pools do not flow fast; the water seems much darker and more stagnant. There are grass and reed banks – plenty of obvious places to drop your fly – and stones, both underwater and exposed, but no shade or shelter. Fishing it, either the rise is general, or there is none. Also, it sometimes comes on and goes off several times during an afternoon.

It requires very delicate wading, cautious and slow; otherwise you will hardly see a fish. They tend to lie all over the river, but with a preponderance, all the same, at the sides. At each pool I step in carefully, walk to the middle of it very slowly, then stand still for a time before fishing, spotting movements and considering how to fight the wind. The fish take very quietly indeed here, more so, I think, than almost anywhere else in the river, and as usual the bigger the fish, the smaller the fuss.

The top pool of the series is a fine one. It starts shallow and fast-flowing with a rocky bank on the left-hand side; you fish it from the right. Then it narrows, the current keeping to the left, flowing rapidly for fifteen yards. Along the right bank is a backwater. As usual, I fish the backwater, at the edge of the current. It is a deep pool, to be watched for five minutes before fishing, for the big trout in it are cautious, and more easily caught when they have been observed. Nevertheless I get one of them only every few years.

It is at this point that you become conscious of James Buchanan's Distillery with its strange umbrella-topped chimneys. The bitter-sweet, slightly rank smell of the burnt ale catches your nostrils in the evening as you fish. Some hate it, but for me it has a dash of newness which is pleasant after a day of straightforward, identifiable natural smells, all or most of them easily linked to their origins. The distillery puzzles you the first time you smell it.

Here, too, the hotel is in sight. There is a small temptation when parched or tired to pack up and take the road home. Grey and chunky, beside its conifer spinney, backed by the hills, it beckons delightfully; but I follow the river.

It turns to the right, and for two hundred yards there is broken water that I tell myself for form's sake contains very few trout. The village rubbish dump lies near the stream, and I use this as my excuse for giving this stretch only scant attention. I make few casts in fact before the bed of the distillery burn meets the river on the right bank. It is not even a wraith of the burn it used to be. All the water has been tapped above the distillery and piped to Loch Ericht. This is one of the main reasons why the Truim runs so low in the summer and why possibly, one day, the fishing will diminish and fail.

Above the burn entry, in full sight of the distillery and the road, there is a smooth pool thirty or so yards long, deep and bordered on its right bank with rushes. It is another pool to be waded cautiously. The secret of taking fish in it is to use Olives until you reach the end of the smooth water, then in the ten-yard run at the top change to the smallest of Black Nymphs. It is worth the change because at least one big trout always lives at the top of the pool, and over the years I have found out that the Nymph is what they feed on.

I clamber out, clattering over the rocks, keeping to the left bank to fish the small hole above it, in which I have watched what must now be a very big trout for several years. The fly drags, fishing from either bank, and this well-informed and wise fish can easily be seen throughout his length, inspecting my fly as it goes past and rejecting it with nice judgement. It is at least a ritual to try for him, and I always do it for a moment, then turn with the stream to the right to the long broken pool just below the road as it passes the distillery. This pool is full of snags and the jetsam of an inhabited place: tin cans, old motor tyres, parts of iron bedsteads; a catholic selection. But there is generally at least one good fish waiting here, like Johnny Town Mouse, if you can find him and keep him clear of the snags after you hook him.

After it the river turns left, and serpentines home to the hotel over the fields, past the railway station, past the village, less than a hundred yards from it at one point, to the pool in the very back garden of the hotel itself, with its concrete barrier and seething clear water.

People have said to me, local people and people on visits to Dalwhinnie, that it takes an optimist to fish a burn in the middle of a village. They remember their childhood and playing in the pools, or if they come from somewhere else, notice how inhabited and frequented the riverside is. Besides, the stream is narrow and growing narrower all the time. Its very smallness discourages the incompletely informed and the unobservant.

The fact is, however, that the river here is to be fished carefully. It is not every day that it receives anyone's attention, being protected by over-familiarity and nearness. The water is exceedingly clear, and the bottom has more gravel to it than in other parts of the river. It is perhaps a shade more unpardoning of cast shadows than elsewhere, because the cast shadow spells danger and is better known to the trout than in the lonelier parts of the stream. I simply walk more cautiously, stand farther back, and land my fly, if the wind allows it, more lightly than ever. Curiously, the fish tend to be more out in the stream here than in at the bank; though one still fishes the water, with application and inspired guesswork, rather than the scant rises. On the best days, when there is plenty of water, I have been known to pick up three fine fish on this village stretch on the way home, for there are half a dozen pools and small runs as good as many that are farther away and look more promising. I think I have a developed instinct for fishing on my own doorstep, because I remember how completely people tend to reject the familiar merely because it is familiar.

14

THE LAST POOL

The last pool of the Truim, the pool of which I have spoken as being in the back garden of the hotel itself, is of course not the last pool. Above it, as the valley narrows, the Truim grows smaller, but not less pretty. One can go on from the hotel for several miles. There is the pool at the dam, between a quarter and half a mile up, and the pools at the bridges beyond it. The banks have been marked by my footsteps.

But to end this river portrait in what I have come to look upon as my own back garden is no bad idea.

I have fished up to the hotel many times, soaking wet, tired out and cold to the inner marrow, but I fish the 'last pool' with nostalgic regret at the end of every day. I stand in the water listening to the sounds of living in the hotel and see people at the windows watching me as I cast, and play with the fly, making it dance on the water to my own rhythm. Somebody comes out from the kitchen and speaks to me, and I answer; I hear voices from inside the house and from the bar. Chickens scratch on the nettled green bank; a dog barks. The smell of smoke is in the air.

I recall the people of the house who have gone since I knew it, the dearly-loved, capable, upright, and warm-hearted Mrs Matheson senior who used to see me through the kitchen window as I fished the pool and put on a little wonder for me, like a girl, when I came in and showed her my catch. Mrs Kinnear, who works now with Ian Matheson at Loch Duich, I remember for her constant care of me, her tempered amazement at my wetness and disorder, and her acceptance and partial control of it while I was under her jurisdiction. Many guests who loved the place grew old and then, one season, unexpectedly, were no longer there. Dr Wight who, when I came in with a fine fish on a Sunday, would turn his eyes to the ceiling, and declare with round mock piety, 'Well, the better the day, the better the deed!' The pink-faced old gentleman who recited Burns and Wordsworth as he ate his breakfast porridge, dipping his spoon in a cup of cold milk, which he held under his chin. Sandy MacEwan, with his solemn wit, who once started an absurd enchanting reminiscence by saying, 'I remember during the First World War, when we were in camp on the Crianlarich side of Baghdad . . .'

The hotel is inhabited by many familiar, excellent ghosts, as well as guests.

But there is always the new season for whoever is there, for whoever can stand its vagaries without criticism and without disappointment. The fact is that on the Truim, in many ways, I have known my heart's desire, recognized and rejoiced in it, and have sung and shouted for pleasure because of that recognition. This happens to few people about any subject, and is to be marvelled at. May you not be led too far astray by this most prejudiced book. The Truim is no less a hard little burn for having been greatly praised.